HOAXES AND HEXES

Daring Deceptions and Mysterious Curses

BARBARA SMITH

D0089328

HERITAGE

VICTORIA · VANCOUVER · CALGARY

Heritage House Publishing Company Ltd.
www.heritagehouse.ca

Library and Archives Canada Cataloguing in Publication
Smith, Barbara, 1947–
    Hoaxes and hexes: daring deceptions and famous frauds / Barbara Smith.

(Amazing stories)
Issued also in electronic format.
ISBN 978-1-926613-98-7

   1. Hoaxes. 2. Swindlers and swindling. 3. Impostors and imposture. I. Title. II. Series: Amazing stories (Surrey, B.C.)

CT9980.S65 2011   001.9'5   C2011-900359-7

Series editor: Lesley Reynolds.
Cover design: Chyla Cardinal. Interior design: Frances Hunter.
Cover photo: MDK Graphics/iStockphoto.

 The interior of this book was printed on 100% post-consumer recycled paper, processed chlorine free and printed with vegetable-based inks.

Heritage House acknowledges the financial support for its publishing program from the Government of Canada through the Canada Book Fund (CBF), Canada Council for the Arts and the province of British Columbia through the British Columbia Arts Council and the Book Publishing Tax Credit.

14 13 12 11   1 2 3 4 5
Printed in Canada

For S.G. and R.R. with thanks,
and for Bob, Debbie and Robyn—
from beginning to end

Contents

Prologue

THE PIRATE CAPTAIN CALLED OUT *a warning: "Heave to,*
SS Moyie, and prepare to be boarded!" Oddly, the threatened
paddlewheeler didn't try to make a run for it but slowed in
response to the command.

This would be a profitable heist. The pirates aboard the
Tyrant Queen *would steal the passengers' valuables, of course,*
but the real prize was the payroll that Bill Henson, a career
pirate, had said would be on board.

All was going exactly as planned—but then it should.
Gunpowder Gertie, the Pirate Queen, knew what to expect.
She'd raided dozens of paddlewheelers in her day. But as she
scanned the other ship's deserted deck, icicles of suspicion snaked
down her spine. Something was wrong—very wrong. The Moyie

appeared deserted. There wasn't a person in sight. And what was that glint of metal?

In the blink of an eye, dozens of armed policemen stood where there should have been wealthy passengers. Gertie knew she was badly outgunned. She barely heard the police chief order "Fire!" before she turned tail. Bullets whizzed through the air and slammed into the pirate ship—the ship that Gunpowder Gertie had stolen from those same policemen five years before.

Were her days of ruling British Columbia's inland waterways over? Was she going to die? It all could have been so different. If only that avalanche hadn't killed her mother . . .

No time now for regrets. Bullets rained down all around her. She had to get away. The Tyrant Queen's *engines howled under the strain, then an explosion blew a gaping hole in the ship. Gunpowder Gertie, the Pirate Queen, had been sabotaged.*

"Bill Henson, you traitor!" she screamed as shrapnel flew through the air and her ship began to sink.

But Gunpowder Gertie didn't die that day. As a matter of fact, in an odd way, that blazing gun battle was only the beginning of the Pirate Queen's amazing story.

Introduction

THE OXFORD CONCISE ENGLISH DICTIONARY defines a "hoax" as a "humorous or malicious deception; a practical joke" and a "hex" as "a spell" or a "curse." But dictionary definitions can't come close to doing justice to these intriguing reflections of human nature. Let's look at the phenomenon of hoaxes first.

Creating a hoax requires considerable ingenuity and effort, so why bother? Clearly, anyone motivated to set up a hoax must believe there's at least the possibility of some sort of benefit. Sometimes the motivation is entirely innocent, as was the case when Carolyn McTaggart told a group of children about Gunpowder Gertie, Pirate Queen of the Kootenays and Canada's only known female pirate.

Few hoaxes begin that innocently, though. No doubt get-rich-quick schemes date back to a cave dweller promising beachfront underground homes to another tribe. Sadly, judging by stock-market hoaxes, not much has changed. Usually, however, a hoax is neither so innocent nor so evil but merely reflects our curious desire to believe in the impossible, such as the remains of a giant found in a field near Lillooet, BC, or a homemade submarine crossing the Atlantic Ocean.

Hoaxes can be complicated, but how complex would it be if there was such a thing as a hexed hoax? The Mitchell-Hedges crystal skull is purported to be an example of exactly that. Once owned by Canadian Anna Mitchell-Hedges, this exquisitely crafted artifact was supposedly made 4,000 years ago—and it's said to be cursed!

There are many hexes in the world of sports and entertainment. Hollywood's hex on the best actress Oscar winner originated in 1929 with Canadian actress Mary Pickford, and there have been many others affected since. The skills of Saskatchewan-born hockey player Mark Messier were necessary to lift a curse on Madison Square Garden. The LaBonte curling curse is also international in nature: it was named after an American, originated in Germany and involved a Canadian team.

Whether or not you believe in hoaxes or hexes, they are actual parts of our history—unless we've all been hoaxed!

1

Famous Hoaxes

Real Relics?

Sometimes a day that starts out in the most ordinary of ways can end up being life changing. And occasionally the ripples from such a day reach out and affect many others. This was certainly the case for James Edward Dodd on May 24, 1931.

Dodd lived in northern Ontario and worked as a brakeman for the Canadian National Railway. In his spare time he enjoyed prospecting for gold. Given that combination of circumstances, it's not surprising that Dodd often explored land adjacent to railway tracks. On that particular spring Sunday, his quest for treasure took him to a spot near Beardmore, just east of Lake Nipigon's south shore, setting in motion a series of events that rewrote Canadian history books.

As Dodd worked away probing the soil, his trowel hit something solid. Curious, he carefully freed the object—an intriguing and very old-looking piece of metal. He set to work loosening the surrounding dirt, and soon he was holding four oddly shaped pieces of metal that he incorrectly presumed were remnants of a long-ago Native encampment. Intrigued, he brought the items home, stashed them in his basement and promptly forgot about them.

Some months later, Dodd's wife came across the rusty old fragments in the basement and made it more than clear that she did not want such trash in the house. Dodd was happy to oblige. After all, the articles weren't tremendously important to him; yet, he couldn't bear to part with them completely. He put them out in the woodshed.

Word of Dodd's unusual find eventually spread from one person to another, until by 1936, Dr. Charles Currelly, the first director of Toronto's Royal Ontario Museum (ROM) had heard of them. Currelly was intrigued enough to ask Dodd to bring the relics to Toronto for examination. At the museum, an expert revealed that these were not Native artifacts but Norse relics. More precisely, they were two pieces of a broken sword, the head of an axe or a spear and a fourth piece that was believed to have been part of a shield. The kicker was that these objects dated from roughly 980 AD. The historical implications were undeniably staggering.

The museum purchased the relics from Dodd for $500 (a substantial sum during the Depression) and proudly displayed them. Here was definitive proof that Norse explorers had made their way much farther inland than anyone had previously suspected. Canada's history had been virtually rewritten, all thanks to an amateur prospector's chance find.

Dr. Currelly submitted articles for publication in scholarly journals describing the museum's acquisitions, while magazines and newspapers of the day detailed the events for the general public. This was a hotly discussed topic, but interestingly, not everyone who entered into the discussions had respect for James Edward Dodd's integrity.

By the mid-1950s, the relics had been on display at the ROM for nearly 20 years. The theory that Norse explorers had travelled well into the interior of the North American continent before 1000 AD had become widely accepted. Canadian author and popular historian Farley Mowat linked the find at Beardmore to the runestones discovered in Kensington, Minnesota. People flocked to lectures describing this absolute proof that a Norseman had died in Ontario over 900 years earlier. All in all, there was considerable excitement.

Unfortunately, the truth behind the relics was considerably less exciting, and that truth was about to surface. Walter Dodd, James' son, went public with an announcement that his father had absolutely *not* stumbled across the relics while prospecting near train tracks in May 1931. Instead, the older man had found them in the basement of a Port Arthur (now Thunder Bay) house.

It's likely that James Dodd knew, or at least suspected, that the relics themselves were genuine Norse artifacts—which they are—but he either had a flair for the dramatic or thought that a more unlikely context would somehow enhance their value. As if this deceit wasn't bad enough, it was rumoured that certain senior staff members at the ROM had long been suspicious of the claim's accuracy. By the late 1950s, the fraudulent exhibit had been removed.

Today the artifacts, including their complete and corrected history, are back on display at the ROM. Their provenance has been traced to Scandinavian immigrants who came to Canada in 1923.

The hoax might have been embarrassing for the ROM, but it did acquire genuine Norse artifacts for only $500, and the fabrication was revealed for what it was before any northern Ontario sports teams changed their names to the Vikings!

Like Father, Like Son

As you may remember from elementary school, the great explorer Giovanni Caboto was an Italian who, when it suited his purpose, became John Cabot, a great English explorer. More diligent social studies teachers might also have mentioned that Giovanni, or John (depending on what year it was), was the proud father of three sons, although we would have only learned about the middle lad, Sebastian (1484–1557), because even in their lifetimes, his brothers Lewis and Sancio didn't get a lot of press.

Sebastian, though, had an industrious streak and followed along in his father's footsteps, so to speak. It's a shame that there wasn't time in school curricula for minutiae, because Sebastian Cabot led a fascinating life, and he was truly one of the most fortunate of men. He lived long enough to fulfill all of his dreams—and then some.

From the early 1500s on, the younger Cabot was so revered for his record-fast cross-Atlantic voyages to the New World that he and they were spoken of in hushed tones. His exploration accomplishments set the standard by which all others would be judged for many years, and his opinions on the search for a westerly route to China were sought by the leaders of many countries. It was no wonder; Sebastian Cabot's expertise was born of a lifetime of solid experience, and it was fitting that he lived out the last years of his life in comfort and dignity.

It all began in 1497, when Sebastian wasn't much more than a boy. He and his brothers accompanied their father on his ship *Matthew*. The expedition was small and poorly financed, and the departure of the Cabots and 15 other men from the English port city of Bristol didn't attract much attention. Three months later, however, the group returned as conquering heroes. They had landed on North American soil! England's King Henry VII was so impressed that the following year His Royal Highness granted John Cabot substantial funding to make a second journey, this one consisting of several ships and some 300 men.

Of course, being a seafaring man in the 16th century was an extremely dangerous occupation, and sadly, John Cabot didn't survive that second trip. From the facts that remain, it's presumed that he died somewhere near Newfoundland. Interestingly, the names of his older and younger sons, Lewis and Sancio, also passed from public records at that point. Sebastian, however, not only lived to tell of that voyage but also to make his own considerable impact on the world—an impact that historians debate to this day because, strangely, early 16th-century English mariners were not meticulous record-keepers, unlike Italian, Portuguese or Spanish seafarers. Information about Sebastian Cabot's next historic trip, in 1508, must be pieced together from notes of interviews granted by Cabot when he was an elderly man. According to those sources, Cabot apparently crossed the Atlantic in record-breaking time, landed on the banks of the island now known as Newfoundland and from there turned north, searching for what all explorers of that era sought: the elusive northern passage through North America.

From Cabot's descriptions it was presumed that the convoy sailed into the mouth of Hudson Bay and would have pushed on even farther but for the frigid winter conditions. His men were so cold that they were threatening mutiny. Wisely, Cabot turned the ships around and headed south. They very likely wintered near Florida. By April 1509, the adventurers were back home in Bristol with tales to tell.

With his compass and globe, Sebastian Cabot looks every inch the dignified and accomplished mariner in this portrait.

In return, the English royal family had tales to tell Cabot. Henry VII had died, and his son, Henry VIII, was now the country's ruler. This had decidedly discouraging implications for any man calling himself an explorer, because Henry VIII had no interest in financially supporting their expeditions.

While that news might have been disappointing to Sebastian, there were a couple of interesting spinoffs from the situation. For one thing, with his father and possibly both of his brothers now dead, Sebastian was effectively the only exploring Cabot in town. And with no further expeditions being made, young Cabot's stories were the most recent ones available to anyone intrigued by voyages across the Atlantic. Predictably, those stories improved with each telling, and apparently Sebastian not only encouraged the misinformation but added to it. One would think that skeptics would have questioned yarns that claimed he had sailed with a crew of 300 in two ships, but people were clearly not willing to see Sebastian Cabot for what he was: the era's biggest con man. He adopted and adapted his father's accomplishments to his own purposes, which significantly increased his standing in the world of mariners. By the early 1500s, if John Cabot was remembered at all, it was as a lowly merchant.

Then, as interest renewed in the search for a westerly route to China, Sebastian worked the angles again. Within a matter of months he had effectively become the go-to guy for the competing governments of Portugal, Spain, England and Venice in matters of marine navigation.

But Sebastian Cabot was not one to rest on his ill-gotten reputation, and in 1526, when he was close to 50 years of age, he embarked on a voyage to what is now South America. Funded by Spanish investors, the trip lasted four years and left a substantial paper trail of lawsuits filed against him by his crew and his benefactors.

Cabot reached his destination but tales of gold and silver not far inland enticed him away from his mission of searching for a passage through the continent. Some of his men threatened to mutiny, so he abandoned them. Then, when his ship ran aground, Captain Cabot was the first to jump to safety. He encouraged 30 of his sailors to accompany Native guides, who led them directly into a deadly ambush.

By 1528, even Cabot knew he was in deep trouble. He sent one of his ships back to Spain to ask for assistance. This request was categorically denied, and it was another two years before the motley crew that remained in Sebastian Cabot's beleaguered armada made it back to Seville, Spain.

As soon as he stepped foot off his ship, Cabot was accused of so many counts of mismanagement and disobedience that the hearing took years to work its way through the judicial system. He was found guilty, fined heavily and banished to Morocco—a terrible way to end a remarkable career—except that he never served any part of his sentence. Instead, he immediately returned to his position as a maritime consultant, and when he died in 1557, he was still a much-admired man.

Interestingly, there is no record of where his body was laid to rest. His reputation, however, has not been laid to rest at all, for most historians believe that the only voyage Sebastian Cabot led was the disastrous one to South America in 1526. According to scholarly research, it is very doubtful that he left dry land in either 1508 or 1509; he appears to have merely described his father's earlier voyages, changed the dates and taken credit for them himself. He may not even have been aboard the *Matthew* for its historic voyage. The implications are daunting—despite having little experience at sea, Cabot spent most of his life being well paid to advise navigators (from competing countries) who were undertaking life-threatening voyages across the Atlantic Ocean.

As for the esteem he enjoyed toward the end of his life, it's clear that although he may have been treated with great deference, he certainly had no integrity, and although he may have enjoyed the respect of others, he certainly hadn't earned it. Sebastian Cabot was little more than a con artist and an extremely good or extremely lucky hoaxer. Of course, such inclinations might have been genetic, considering he was fathered by a Venetian named Giovanni Caboto but raised as an Englishman from Bristol by the more suitably named John Cabot.

A Giant Hoax

Some hoaxes are so cleverly set up that even after it's been revealed that they're scams, they maintain an aspect of plausibility. Other hoaxes are so obvious that it's hard to believe anyone could ever have been gullible enough to have believed in them.

The following tale certainly fits squarely in the latter category, but even so, the story rated nearly a full-page spread in the *Vancouver Sun*'s September 2, 1944, edition. An artist named Wilson illustrated the article, in which journalist Albert Foote recollects a truly fantastic find in a farm field near Lillooet, BC. It seems that way back in 1912, as a rancher was plowing a section of his land, his blade hit something very solid.

The man scrambled to see how he could clear away the object before it damaged his plow. Unfortunately, it appeared that this was going to be a tough fix because what he found was "a ten-foot solid petrified early day resident of the province." Yes, buried just below soil level was a completely intact specimen of a prehistoric giant.

Needless to say, the farmer was aghast. He ran to a neighbour's house pleading that the other man come and see his incredible find. Before too long, word spread, and soon a crowd formed. The landowner quickly assured everyone gathered there that although he was sure he could make a tidy profit if he sold this amazing specimen "to a circus or a museum," he was far too moral a man to do such a thing.

Instead he would "cover this giant up again and let him rest peaceful-like." The rancher further urged those who had gathered to view this enormous fossil not to say a word to anyone about the find.

Of course it was a little late for that caution. As a matter of fact, writer Albert Foote reported that "within twenty-four hours, the astounding news had been flashed around the globe." It wasn't long, according to the 1944 article, before an opportunistic American promoter from Georgia "shoved a contract, accompanied by a hundred-dollar bill, under [the rancher's] nose." From that moment on, the gigantic, calcified corpse belonged to the American.

Next, at what must have been tremendous expense, the relic was moved to a vacant store on Vancouver's Cordova Street where, for only 25 cents each, members of the public could view "one of God's earliest experiments in biology." As long as those viewers were adult males, that is, for a huge banner declared "men only."

Despite that proviso, the lineup to see the great oddity stretched for blocks. It seemed that everyone was interested. Some of those who were most interested, however, were physicians. These doctors thought that a thorough post-mortem examination was in order. The popular exhibit was shut down while the procedure was carried out. It wasn't long before the medical practitioners announced their findings in a terse declaration. The gigantic petrified prehistoric specimen wasn't even close to being human, nor had it ever been. "The image is composed of concrete."

The American promoter was charged with obtaining money under false pretenses, but there's no record of what, if anything, happened to the rancher who supposedly discovered the behemoth. Of course, that part of the story could have been as manufactured as the prehistoric giant himself.

There's little doubt that this giant was a direct and equally fraudulent descendant of the Cardiff Giant, whose owner, William Newell, successfully toured with his creation in the 1860s. When the giant corpse was eventually found to be a fake, it was termed "the world's greatest hoax."

The Great Gunpowder Gertie

In 1879, George and Violet Stubbs celebrated the birth of a beautiful baby girl at their home in an English port town. They named their daughter Gertrude Imogen, and when she was 16, the little family emigrated to Canada—to Sandon, BC, to be precise.

Not long after, a natural disaster struck the town. High up on a south-facing slope of the Selkirk Mountains, a stone fell. That stone's fall freed a rock from its precarious perch, and that in turn loosened a boulder from the niche it had been wedged into for centuries. As the boulder fell, it crashed against another, cracking it and jarring an enormous sheet of stone. Soon, in a thunderous demonstration of the law of gravity, other stones, rocks and boulders tumbled free and an avalanche pounded the fledgling town.

Repercussions from that avalanche set in motion a decidedly unnatural series of events in Gertrude's life, for it killed her mother, and the older woman's death utterly devastated her father. He couldn't cope with the loss of his wife and, in an attempt to ease his pain, began drinking heavily. Less than a year later, Gertrude was an orphan, alone and vulnerable in a new country.

After assessing and immediately rejecting the obvious options for a young woman in her circumstances, the girl decided to pursue a non-traditional career path. She turned to a life of crime. Gertrude Imogen Stubbs became Gunpowder Gertie, Pirate Queen of the Kootenays.

A basic tool of the piracy trade is, of course, a pirate ship, and that was something Gunpowder Gertie lacked—until she managed to "liberate" a 42-foot-long cruiser from the British Columbia Provincial Police. Her first order of business was to change the vessel's name from *Witch* to *Tyrant Queen*. That seemingly simple act subtly but effectively demonstrated how ill-prepared the up-and-coming thief was for her new endeavour. As anyone with any nautical knowledge knows, changing the name of a boat can bring bad luck. Surprisingly, it took five years for that jinx to catch up with Gertie, and by the time it did, she'd already made profitable use of the former police boat by raiding passenger and cargo ships as they sailed the Kootenay River system.

Of course, pirates don't work alone, because part of their effectiveness lies in outnumbering those they prey upon. This meant that Gunpowder Gertie had to assemble a like-minded crew, and therein lies one of the great risks of any criminal enterprise: the people she hired were, by definition, crooks. Of course, the police knew this and decided to take advantage of the fact. They approached Bill Henson, one of Gertie's deckhands aboard the *Tyrant Queen*, and struck a deal with him. If Henson agreed to help them apprehend Gunpowder Gertie, there'd be a generous reward in it for him. The lawmen's ploy was successful, and within a matter of days Canada's only known female pirate was serving a life sentence in prison.

According to Gertie's biographer, Carolyn McTaggart, Gertrude Imogen Stubbs, the woman once known as the Pirate Queen of the Kootenays, died in prison "of pneumonia during the terrible winter of 1912."

Now any Canadian worthy of their maple leaf would just shake their head when they came across this story for the first time. If there are such interesting stories in our country's history, why are we only taught the boring ones in school? And that's exactly what the producers of the CBC radio program *This Day in History* thought. In the late 1990s, they created and aired a show to give Canada's female pirate the acknowledgement they felt she deserved. Unfortunately, there was a serious flaw in their research: "Gunpowder Gertie" never existed. She was a hoax—

admittedly the kindest and most well-meaning of hoaxes, but a hoax nonetheless.

Amateur historian Carolyn McTaggart wanted to make local history engaging for a group of youngsters. Toward that end, she invented both Gertrude Imogen Stubbs and her alter ego, Gunpowder Gertie. Then McTaggart set the fictitious character amid factual events and totally captivated her young charges.

Now McTaggart was creative but not irresponsible, so after the lesson she carefully explained to the children which parts of the story had been make-believe and which had not. Apparently, though, not all the children reported that addendum to their parents, and that set into motion a series of events that resulted in the embarrassingly inaccurate radio show.

Since then, this hoax has been so embraced by the people of the district that it has become a fond part of the area's history. A local newspaper ran the story to great effect on April Fool's Day, and Carolyn McTaggart has told the tall tale to enthusiastic audiences at various storytelling festivals. A mock-up of Gunpowder Gertie's ship *Tyrant Queen* has even been a float in a parade!

Gertrude Imogen Stubbs might not have come to British Columbia in 1895, but once she did get here, via Carolyn McTaggart's imagination roughly a century later, her story certainly took its place in our history.

Solo in a Sub?

On a fine summer day early in August 1966, fishermen near the French coastal city of Brest spotted something floating in the water. After manoeuvring their boat closer to the object, they were shocked to see that it was a life raft—an occupied life raft. The man in the raft was barely coherent and covered with lacerations. The fishermen pulled the struggling survivor into their boat and quickly made for shore.

They likely found the man's clothing a bit odd, as he was wearing an aviator's helmet and goggles. But his unusual style of dress paled in comparison to the story he was about to tell. The injured man explained to his rescuers that he had travelled across the Atlantic Ocean from Canada in a homemade submarine! He claimed that he'd made the trip solo and that it had taken him a mere 13 hours.

As soon as the fishing boat reached land, the rescuers took their unusual catch to a doctor. After the injured man's wounds were tended, he was questioned by French authorities, who were most interested in his story. The survivor identified himself as 36-year-old Josef Papp. He explained that he'd been living in Canada since fleeing his home in Hungary a few months after the revolution in 1956.

Papp went on to say that he was an engineer by training but an inventor by inclination and that he had invented and built a fusion-powered submarine. He'd made this cross-Atlantic trip of 3,500 kilometres in order to test his invention. Aside from a stability issue, the sub had performed well, Papp maintained. He'd even reached the mind-boggling underwater speed of 480 kilometres per hour. Unfortunately for those anxious to examine this amazing vessel, Papp explained that he'd destroyed the sub as soon as he'd reached Europe because he didn't want his invention to fall into enemy hands.

At first glance it would seem a terrible shame that such a potentially revolutionary device had been destroyed. Surely the world could have profited by the technology Papp claimed to have developed. With closer examination, however, it also seemed an awfully convenient coincidence that there was no submarine to examine, especially if Mr. Papp was the type of man who might be prone to exaggeration. And apparently that was exactly the type of man he was—that and a few other things too; "paranoid," "unstable," "selfish," "unpredictable," "a fraud" and "a liar" were a few other descriptors that had been assigned to the man in the past.

Interestingly, a background check revealed that Papp had actually met with some success as an inventor. He had three patents registered with the United States government, all having to do with energy technology. It was also known that he'd built an experimental engine. Tragically, this fact was well documented because on the machine's trial run it had exploded, killing one witness and badly injuring several others.

Who was Josef Papp? Was he deluded or was he perhaps an

eccentric genius? Could he have stumbled across something astounding—something with the potential to change our world? This possibility had to be investigated. And it was.

Unfortunately for those optimistic about the future of underwater travel, one of the first things authorities found was an envelope stuffed in Papp's coat pocket. Inside that envelope were tickets: one was the return portion of a flight between Montreal and Paris. The other was a train ticket from Paris to the coastal community of Brest, near where Papp had been picked up by the fishermen.

In the end, it was widely accepted that Josef Papp had not travelled across the Atlantic Ocean in a homemade submarine but had flown to Paris and from there made his way to the spot where he was found. His motivation for the ruse seemed to be a rather pathetic attempt to save face with the scientific community after his first trial had literally blown up and ended in tragedy.

Not surprisingly, Papp's attempted hoax failed completely, and by the time of his death from cancer in 1989, the bizarre inventor was largely forgotten. Despite this, records of his complex theories still exist and actually have something of a cult following. He wrote a book, *The Fastest Submarine, 300 MPH Plus!*, describing his accomplishments and endeavours. It was published in the United States by Ballantyne Books, a large and reputable company. The volume is long out of print but has become a highly prized collector's item among Josef Papp's followers.

The truth about a person's accomplishments in life is, it seems, open to interpretation.

A Clear-Headed Mystery

In 1924, when Anna Mitchell-Hedges was a girl of 17, she and her father, Mike, left their home in Port Colborne, Ontario, to begin the long trek to Lubaantum, Belize. This wasn't a holiday the pair was embarking on; nonetheless they were looking forward to the trip with delighted anticipation—and it's no wonder. After all, they hoped to discover Atlantis!

Although they didn't find the lost city, the journey was a tremendous success for both Anna and her father. So successful, in fact, that it changed Anna's life forever. As she explained many times after they returned, while examining a Mayan archaeological site, she had made a sensational discovery: a rock crystal skull.

The skull was nearly 4,000 years old, she informed people. It had taken generations of Native artisans over 150 years to carve the piece, which stood about 10 centimetres high and even had a moveable jawbone. Anna was utterly thrilled to be in possession of this unique artifact. Oddly though, her father once publicly referred to the skull as being "the embodiment of all evil."

Interestingly, after her father's death in 1959, Anna changed her story about the history of the skull, maintaining that, in fact, it hadn't been carved by Native artisans at all but had actually come from outer space before being transported from Atlantis to Belize for safekeeping. Anna claimed that the crystal skull was endowed with supernatural abilities. It sometimes made ominous growls and chants, while at other times it gave off light. The differences were apparently dependent upon how the planets were aligned at that time. Strangely, Anna Mitchell-Hedges even boasted once that she'd used the skull's powers to kill a man.

Now, the Mitchell-Hedges skull was not the only crystal skull in the world. There were others, and they were all said to be imbued with supernatural powers. Some were even credited with miraculous healing properties, an opposite claim to Anna's allegations of murder-by-skull.

The mythology surrounding the existence of crystal skulls does reinforce the assertions of mystical powers. Some people maintain that they have seen images of people or events in the crystal, while others hold that there are a total of 13 skulls in the world and that in the year 2012 the skulls will all be gathered in one place and some enigmatic power will be released. Since there are known to be far more than 13 crystal skulls in the world, this last prediction is no longer considered much of a threat.

The entire mythology surrounding the skulls is fascinating, but it is also extremely suspect, and Anna's stories were improbable right from the moment she supposedly found the skull. There are numerous photographs taken of both Anna and her father on their expedition in 1924, and yet not one picture includes the skull. Nor was it mentioned in either of the journals in which they recorded detailed inventories. The other explorers who were on that expedition don't remember any mention of the discovery of a crystal skull during that trip to Belize.

It's likely that Mitchell-Hedges altered her story about the skull's creation when scientists determined that the diamond-tipped power tools needed to craft such a piece weren't invented until the 20th century. She might have believed that suggesting the skull came from outer space was a way to skirt that issue, making it impossible to disprove her assertion. Of course, the opposite is also true—it's impossible to *prove* that it came from outer space.

As rock crystal contains no carbon, it can't be carbon dated, and so there's no way to verify its age. By now, however, most people believe that the original crystal skulls, including the Mitchell-Hedges skull, were carved by European craftsmen in the late 1800s, using crystal from South America. It's widely suspected that Mike and Anna Mitchell-Hedges actually purchased the skull in 1943 at an auction.

To date, no one has been able to categorically prove that the Mitchell-Hedges skull is or is not a hoax. What is known for certain is that Anna Mitchell-Hedges kept the odd artifact with her until her death in 2007 at the age of 100 and that she left explicit instructions for its care. The skull continues to be carefully guarded by Bill Homann, the man who was Anna's guardian during the last years of her life.

2

Great Frauds and Swindlers

Black Gold or Black Heart?

In the months leading up to the outbreak of the First World War, Calgary, Alberta, was a thriving city of roughly 55,000 souls—many with entrepreneurial hearts beating in their chests. Some of those go-getters had helped to form the 100,000 Club, an organization dedicated to the lofty goal of seeing their city's population grow to that six-digit figure. In a nutshell, you simply couldn't have thrown a stone across Stephen Avenue without hitting a capitalist or two, and insurance salesman George Edward Buck, recently arrived in Calgary from Toronto, was most assuredly one of those.

Buck might have had his fill of chasing folks for their

insurance premiums, because he also changed professions and, once settled in Alberta, headed straight for the pulpit. Among other topics, he preached eloquently about the virtues of buying shares in the Black Diamond Oil Fields Company—a company he happened to own.

For a while, minister Buck enjoyed a substantial income from his parishioners' contributions, but their funds were limited, and eventually those who had purchased shares in his company became understandably restless to see a return on their investment.

Buck was not one to disappoint. After dumping a pail full of oil into his "well," he arranged for a few carefully chosen journalists to view the site. With as much showmanship as he used from his usual spot at the pulpit, he slowly cranked on a pulley. Soon a bucket of thick, black oil rose from the ground. The reporters gasped and hurried to get back to their typewriters. They had a huge story to share with their readers.

The stunt paid off as the ensuing publicity padded Buck's wallet most satisfactorily. That turn of events did, however, complicate the scheme, because now he needed to protect his phony oil well from prying eyes. Toward that end, he dug a ditch around the site and filled it with water. Then, perhaps because stocking the newly created moat with crocodiles wouldn't have been feasible, he arranged for an armed guard to patrol the area around the clock.

Eventually, as a house of cards will, the preacher's ploy fell apart, and he fled to the United States for a fresh start in the oil business. Unfortunately for Buck, the long arm of the Canadian law caught up with him, and he was soon brought back to Calgary, where he was charged with and temporarily convicted of fraud. His lawyer successfully appealed that conviction, though, and George Edward Buck walked out of the courtroom a free but certainly not an innocent man.

Buck's oil-well hoax was one of several perpetrated during that era. In his book *Fool's Gold*, Brian Hutchinson writes of sales kiosks being "installed in [Calgary] hotel lobbies, drugstores and barber shops" in 1913 to hawk stock certificates after a gaggle of wannabe tycoons announced they had struck oil less than 30 miles from the city. People clambered to jump onto that bandwagon. Within days, more than a dozen new oil companies had been formed and millions of dollars had changed hands. It was all to no avail—the best that particular oil well could produce was a pocket of naphtha.

Sadly, anxious or greedy investors never seem to learn. From Toronto's Bay Street to the Vancouver Stock Exchange, every decade of the 20th century has produced fraudsters with various schemes. The 1990s was no exception, for that is when a company registered under the name Bre-X Minerals Ltd. appeared on the scene. The firm's executives offered a unique combination of experience and expertise.

David Walsh, the company's founder and chief executive officer, was 35 years old when he moved from Montreal to Calgary in 1980, with hopes of plying his considerable entrepreneurial skills in Alberta's more welcoming business atmosphere. Unfortunately, Walsh's timing was terrible because the western Canadian economy had just taken a serious turn for the worse.

Interestingly, people who met Walsh often commented that they found him particularly unattractive. He was an overweight, rumpled chain-smoker who spent an inordinate amount of time in an assortment of Calgary bars. Despite those disadvantages, in 1992 Walsh attracted 50-year-old geologist John Felderhof to Bre-X.

Felderhof was also unpopular. Many of those who met him during the course of business reported him to be "arrogant," "aggressive" and generally unfriendly. They also noted that those undesirable personality characteristics didn't fit well with the mining culture.

Number three player in this unlikely trio was Michael de Guzman. He was the youngest and by far the smartest of the group, but by the time he joined Bre-X, he had already accumulated a well-earned reputation for dishonest business dealings.

The trio's odd combination of skills and qualities seemed destined to succeed. On May 6, 1993, Walsh, Felderhof and de Guzman, on behalf of Bre-X, announced news that shook the worlds of mining and investment. Their company had been drilling for gold near the Busang River in the jungles of Indonesia, and the initial extractions looked extremely promising.

The company's shares rose dramatically in value over the next few months, with both sophisticated and less-experienced investors all anxious to obtain a piece of the profits. By March 1996, a Bre-X share that had initially sold for about $2 was worth approximately 200 times that. (Reports on the actual dollar amounts vary from $170 to $280 per share.)

But people with knowledge of gold mining had begun to note that drill samples from the Busang site were being taken in an unorthodox manner. Bre-X executives answered these concerns with increasingly impressive numbers. They had initially determined that there could be an astounding 2 million ounces of gold attainable, but that estimate was now revised to between 30 and 40 million ounces and then to an astronomical 70 million ounces. With each new report, share values increased correspondingly.

Walsh, Felderhof and de Guzman must have thought they'd found a licence to print money. Better still, was there anywhere to go from here but up?

There most assuredly was—and that was down, way down. On March 18, 1997, just before an independent firm contracted by the Indonesian government announced that according to their due diligence investigations the Bre-X gold mine near the Busang River was virtually worthless, Michael de Guzman apparently jumped from a helicopter that was flying him to the mine site.

David Walsh and John Felderhof responded to the

consulting company's revelation very differently than de Guzman. They talked—and talked and talked and talked and talked. Both men adamantly maintained that their business plan and mining methods were sound and simply misunderstood. No matter how much they talked, though, they couldn't dispute the results of Freeport-McMoRan Copper & Gold Inc.'s investigation, which found that the samples Bre-X had produced from the Busang mine had been "salted"; that is, gold dust and even shavings from jewellery had been imported into the drilling cores. Predictably, stock prices plummeted until trading was halted entirely.

De Guzman's badly decomposed body was found four days after his ill-fated helicopter ride. The corpse was identified by a few remaining teeth and one fingerprint, although there are many who believe the body recovered was not that of de Guzman at all. That opinion seemed to be upheld nine years later when one of his ex-wives reported having received a money order from him.

Walsh, who steadfastly maintained his innocence, retreated to Nassau, where he died of an aneurysm brought on by a stroke on June 4, 1998. Felderhof, who also maintains his innocence, was reported to be living in the Philippines.

Despite civil and criminal prosecution, no one has ever been successfully convicted in connection with this horrendous hoax.

A Swindler of International Proportions

Jay Gould was about as flamboyant a financier as you'd ever come across, especially considering he practised his trade a very long time ago, in the late 1800s. Gould, who was born in New York State, demonstrated his energy and industry early on. By the time he was 21, he owned controlling shares in a bank and then began acquiring shares in a railroad. But Gould's ambitions exceeded banking and railroads, and he set out to corner the gold market. Clearly this was a man adept in the ways of entrepreneurship and in judging the character of those he dealt with.

In 1871, however, Gould met his match in a Scottish dignitary who gave his name as Lord Gordon-Gordon. As soon as the Scotsman arrived in the United States, he made his way to Minneapolis, Minnesota, and wasted no time in becoming involved with the local economy. He talked convincingly about land development and backed his words with a $40,000 deposit into a local bank. Needless to say, folks in the young city welcomed him.

In February 1872, Gordon-Gordon moved to New York State, where he announced that he owned a large number of shares of the Erie Railroad—enough that Jay Gould, the president of the railroad, needed Gordon-Gordon's co-operation in order to hold his position. Gordon-Gordon agreed to a temporary partnership of sorts, but his co-operation didn't come cheaply—it cost Gould 20,000 railroad shares, worth nearly $1 million, as well as an additional $200,000 in cash. But, for a while at least, Jay Gould was convinced he'd found a solid compatriot.

Gould's confidence was justifiably shaken, though, when he discovered that Gordon-Gordon had immediately sold the shares he'd been given. In fact, Gould realized he'd been well and truly duped and that the fraud seriously jeopardized his position as president of the railroad. He began legal action against Gordon-Gordon, who by then had fled to Canada, where he would be safe from extradition. To ensure his welcome in Manitoba, he told the appropriate people that he would be contributing to the province's economy through large-scale land development. In short order, Gordon-Gordon was able to settle into a very comfortable life in Winnipeg.

Once Jay Gould and a few of those loyal to him learned where the lordly thief was living, they hurried north and tried to take Gordon-Gordon back to the United States. But because they hadn't entered Canada legally, their plan failed rather spectacularly. Instead of capturing the man they were after, they themselves were captured and incarcerated without bail. The situation became a potentially explosive international incident. Both President Ulysses S. Grant and Prime Minister Sir John A. Macdonald initiated talks to stop an army of Gould's followers from attempting to invade Canada.

The complexities of this international mission attracted enough worldwide attention that a jeweller in Scotland became very interested. From what he read, this man Lord Gordon-Gordon bore a striking resemblance to a man he knew as Lord Glencairn—a man who had stolen tens of thousands of pounds' worth of gems from him. The jeweller's representative, Thomas Smith, came to Canada to investigate and found that, sure enough, Lord Gordon-Gordon and Lord Glencairn were one and the same man. Authorities lost no time in issuing an arrest warrant. The clever imposter's gig was very close to being up, and he knew it.

Perhaps wanting to end his life as flamboyantly as he had lived it, Lord Gordon-Gordon hosted a lavish farewell party in his Winnipeg residence. By all accounts, he enjoyed himself tremendously that evening and gave extravagant gifts to all his guests. Once all the partygoers had departed, their host, the mysterious Lord Gordon-Gordon, killed himself with a single bullet to his head. He died on August 1, 1874.

To this day, no one knows who this creative and prosperous swindler really was. In addition to the names Lord Glencairn and Lord Gordon-Gordon, he had also been known as the Honourable Mr. Herbert Hamilton, George Hubert Gordon and Hubert Campbell Smith, as well as the decidedly odd moniker of Victory Road.

The man's background was no clearer than his name. He might have been the illegitimate son of a minister's son and a family maid, or even the son of the minister himself and the maid. Other research suggests that he was the son of smugglers from the Isle of Jersey. Or, of course, it's possible that neither of these theories are true. It's unlikely we'll ever know anything more about him than we do now—that he was a hoaxer of legendary proportions.

A Money-Making Misery Memoir

Pity the art dealer who buys a forged painting. But what about a book publisher that produces a sensational bestseller that turns out to be nothing more than a pack of lies? James Frey's infamous *A Million Little Pieces*, published by none other than Random House, is only the latest blockbuster to be revealed as a hoax. At first blush, this book just couldn't fail. It had it all: sex, drugs and rock'n'roll. Better still, it was written in an easy-to-read style by the man who'd experienced all the incredible turmoil before rescuing himself and rising like a phoenix from his own ashes.

The book's style fell into a category called a "misery memoir," a genre with a proven track record and therefore virtually guaranteed to be profitable. There was every expectation that Frey's book would sell hundreds of thousands of copies—and it did—at least until this creative endeavour was proven to be a little *too* creative. Random House had been duped. James Frey's *A Million Little Pieces* was not a "misery memoir." It was not a memoir of any sort. It was a hoax.

In the months between publication and revelation, however, those involved made an enormous amount of money. Even after the author's game was up, so to speak, and the details of the hoax had been made public, the book continued to sell astonishingly well.

Frey may have been clever enough to know how to make a fast buck, but he certainly can't be credited with inventing the art of the literary hoax—far from it. Way back in the 1830s, before Canada was even a country, a Canadian woman wrote a misery memoir that made *A Million Little Pieces* read like the feel-good hit of the century. Even the title was sensationalist: *The Awful Disclosures of Maria Monk.*

Maria Monk was born in Quebec. Piecing together what's known of her life, it's reasonable to assume that she was born in either 1816 or 1817, during a time of intense hatred between Protestants and Catholics. Maria's parents were non-practising Protestants who didn't have much interest in ugly international religious debates, but they did have an intense interest in the fact that their daughter's behaviour was out of control. When the girl was 11, they sent her to a Catholic institution. Unfortunately for everyone, Maria's behaviour didn't improve, and she continued to make everyone's lives miserable until she was about 18 years of age and pregnant. The nuns ordered her out.

Maria had nowhere to turn. First her family and now even an institution had renounced her. That would be a frightening situation in any era, but in Montreal in the 1830s, the young woman's choices were severely limited.

Enter William K. Hoyt, a militant Protestant who ran an organization called the Canadian Benevolent Society. It didn't take the zealous Mr. Hoyt long to realize that a racy embellishment of Maria's story could give him ammunition to hurl against the Catholic Church. His excitement over this prospect apparently outweighed his need to be benevolent to any Canadians, because he and Maria immediately moved to New York, where publishers were hungry for as many misery memoirs as they could get, especially if the plots were racy and based in religious controversy. Two such books, *Six Months in a Convent* and *The Nun*, had already sold phenomenally well.

In 1836, *The Awful Disclosures of Maria Monk* hit bookstore shelves. The first printing sold out in no time, and it's no wonder. The book read like a gothic horror story, detailing torture, neglect and cruel punishments almost too terrible to be believed. What inhumane treatment this innocent child had received at the Hotel Dieu at the hands of the Catholic Church! By implication, Maria's words invited her readers to believe that all papists were terrible people.

But wait—this was an entirely different institution than the one that had housed Maria Monk. Further investigation revealed that the Hotel Dieu treated its residents with dignity and respect. Unfortunately, the truth didn't matter; the fraudulent book was an enormous money-maker, and it was time for a sequel.

The second book was cleverly named to tie into the success of the first book. Entitled *Further Disclosures of Maria Monk Concerning the Hotel Dieu Nunnery of Montreal*, it really was just a reprint of everything that had been in the original. The anti-Catholic group with Hoyt at its helm had themselves the beginnings of a profitable franchise.

Next they announced that a woman who'd supposedly been in the institution at the same time as Maria had now come forward to write *her* story, and so a third lurid and dishonest book was published. Spotting a good thing, other firms began publishing their own version of the misery memoir, each book more outrageous than the previous one. Yet again, profit trumped integrity.

It's extremely doubtful that Maria Monk had anything at all to do with writing the first book, but there's even less chance that she had anything to do with the second one. By this time, she'd left Hoyt in New York and had moved to Philadelphia, where a physician named Sleigh had taken her in. By now, though, the sheer momentum of the hoax was enough that the name of Maria Monk was apparently all that was needed to sell thousands of books.

Even Sleigh got on the book bandwagon with a slim volume of his version of Maria's dramatic story. The contents of that effort have been lost to the mists of time, but its mammoth title has been preserved: *An exposure of Maria Monk's pretended abduction and conveyance to the Catholic asylum, Philadelphia by six priests on the night of August 15, 1837: with numerous extraordinary incidents during her residence of six days in this city.* It wasn't exactly a catchy handle, but at least it included the Canadian expatriate's name, and apparently that was all that mattered.

Eventually the books' popularity died down, but not until Maria Monk's daughter had thrown her literary hat into the ring with a book called exactly that—*Maria Monk's Daughter*. Maria died in 1849 at the age of 33. She was destitute. Ironically, reprinted copies of her fraudulent misery memoir are available for sale online for about $20.

Whether or not James Frey's hoax will enjoy equal longevity remains to be known.

3

Daring Imposters

Grey Owl

What excitement! The date December 10, 1937, was sure to go down in history. Imagine—King George VI, his wife, Elizabeth, and their two daughters, the princesses Elizabeth and Margaret, were hosting "a noble red savage," at Buckingham Palace! Surely this was a meeting of diverse cultural icons if there ever was one. At least it would have been except that this "noble red savage" had not travelled *from* his homeland in North America to Buckingham Palace, but was in fact *returning* to his native land.

Archibald Stansfeld Belaney had been born on September 18, 1888, in Hastings, England. By the time he was a toddler, his parents had essentially abandoned him to the care of two maiden aunts. As a boy, Archie, as the lad was fondly known, developed such a fascination with the culture of North America's Wild West that he was virtually obsessed by the subject. He read exhaustively on the topic and then emulated as many Native American ways as he could master, including building teepees in his aunts' garden.

When he was 15, Buffalo Bill Cody's Wild West Show came to Hastings. Archie was thrilled. At last he was able to see first-hand a slice of the life he aspired to. Apparently he was so inspired by the show that just three years later, still a few months shy of his 18th birthday, he boarded a ship bound for Canada. Clearly, Archie was determined to live his dream.

When he arrived in his new homeland, the once-abandoned boy who grew up as Archibald Stansfeld Belaney reinvented himself completely. He told anyone who would listen that he was the son of an Apache mother and a European father. No doubt the latter connection was an attempt to explain away his bright blue eyes.

Archie found work in Temagami, not far from North Bay, Ontario. His paycheque obviously wasn't quite sufficient though, and the following year he returned to England to scrounge for money under the guise of visiting his aunts. The people in Hastings who'd known him before he'd moved to Canada were astounded at the changes they saw in him. Instead of proper English leather shoes, he never wore anything on his feet except moccasins. He'd even changed the way he walked and talked.

Not long after Archie returned to northern Ontario, he met a young woman named Angele Egwuna. While getting to know her, he added even more alterations to his personal history. He told both Angele and her father, an Ojibway chief, that he'd been born in the American southwest and that his father was a Scotsman. His fictional Apache mother, however, remained a constant.

Angele's family liked young Archie very much and took to calling him Wa-Sha-Quon, their name for the grey owl. The literal translation of that phrase is "he who flies by night," and the moniker soon proved to be a more accurate descriptor than his new in-laws could have predicted. In 1910, however, the chief was happy to welcome Grey Owl to his family, and everyone was overjoyed when the chief's first granddaughter arrived the following year. A few months later, Grey Owl walked away from the responsibilities of his wife and child, and he kept on walking for 500 kilometres until he reached Toronto.

By 1912, he had arrived in Biscotasing, Ontario, west of Sudbury, where once again he made friends with the Native population. His fictional heritage was growing even more colourful. According to the story he told this time, he'd been born in Hermosillo, Mexico, to an Apache mother named Katherine Cochise. His father had been a Scotsman who'd served as a Texas Ranger during the Indian Wars.

Not only did Archie now claim to have once been a member of a Wild West show but, oddly, added that he was also a murderer. The killing, he declared, had been an act of altruism; he had killed a Mexican man who'd murdered his father. Unfortunately, he soon made that story of violence somewhat believable when, in a drunken rage, he destroyed the rooming house where he lived. Rather than face the consequences of his actions, Belaney fled from the area, taking Marie Girard, his common-law Metis wife, with him. She was pregnant by then, soon to give birth to Archie's son Johnny, and Archie had the beginnings of a serious drinking problem.

Not long after the outbreak of the First World War, Archie visited the Canadian Army's recruiting office, where he informed them that he had been born in Montreal, was single and that he had once been a member of the Mexican Dragoons. Clearly, fact-checking wasn't the army's highest priority. They needed soldiers, and soon Archie was a sniper. He was held in high regard by both his superiors and his peers, although some of the men later recalled that he had a decidedly odd manner of speaking; his speech sounded exactly like dialogue from a penny-dreadful cowboy-and-Indian novel.

Belaney was injured in combat and taken to an English hospital, where his exotic style of speech and other unique mannerisms were apparently appealing to at least one woman, because he married again early in 1917. Once he'd recuperated sufficiently to travel, he returned to Canada—without his bride.

Belaney had begun dying his hair black and using henna to redden his skin. There is even documentation that he rolled pieces of metal over his nose to flatten it in a further attempt to look more like the Native he claimed to be.

Archie's drinking problem had become a serious addiction by this time. He had been reduced to drinking almost anything he could get his hands on. Liquor was preferable, of course, but vanilla extract, shoe polish or even turpentine served his needs when they had to. Worse, he was a violent drunk, and this made settling in a community for any length of time impossible because he was often run out of town after drunken rampages.

One of those enforced relocations took him back to Temagami where he settled down with his former wife Angele and their daughter, Agnes, who was now a teenager. A year later Angele gave birth to another daughter, Flora, but in keeping with his custom, Belaney left again.

Presumably he continued to make a living through a combination of odd jobs and trapping. Then in 1925, the Ontario government banned non-Natives from trapping for furs. Archie moved to Quebec, where he met the woman he would stay married to for a longer time than any of his other wives. Gertrude Bernard was 18 years his junior, a beautiful, passionate Iroquois woman who had been raised in town and who identified as much with the white settlers as she did with her own people. Grey Owl was smitten. He gave her the pet name Anahareo.

She initially joined him on the traplines, but killing animals other than for food appalled her, and Anahareo soon converted her husband to conservationism, a topic he began to write about and publicly endorse. Archie was rarely seen without his new love and never seen without a bottle of vanilla extract. Despite this, he began writing articles for several periodicals. These pieces were so well received that a publisher asked him to write a book. *The Men of the Last Frontier* was published in 1931 under the name Grey Owl. He now had people's attention.

Soon the federal government appointed him caretaker of Manitoba's Riding Mountain National Park, where he and Anahareo established a beaver colony. Months later they moved on to Saskatchewan's Prince Albert National Park. Here Anahareo gave birth to a daughter, Shirley Dawn, Grey Owl's fourth child.

After a documentary film was made about his work with wildlife preservation, Grey Owl was in demand as a public speaker. It seemed that everyone wanted to hear the wisdom of this "noble savage." By 1935, Grey Owl was receiving international invitations as a lecturer. Although he was only in his 40s, the combination of his war injuries and his continued drinking meant that he was not a well man. Despite this and his demanding schedule on the lecture circuit, he wrote a second book, *Pilgrims of the Wild*, which sold even better than the first one.

In England, people clamoured to see him. Bobbies had to

be called out to control the crowds that gathered to see and hear the "red man" speak. He'd effectively buried his British heritage by proudly and staunchly sticking to his story of being born in Mexico to an Apache mother—even when he spoke in Hastings, where people he'd gone to school with as a child were positive they recognized him.

It's reasonable to assume that he found this duplicity stressful, but if so, he left absolutely no record of it. He did, however, acknowledge that his speaking schedule was gruelling. By the time he sailed back to Canada, he had been touring for four months and had presented hundreds of lectures to thousands of people. Grey Owl was utterly exhausted, a mere shell of his former self. He attempted to recuperate during the voyage home by drinking continuously.

After his return to Canada, he was honoured by Prime Minister William Lyon Mackenzie King and photographed by Yousuf Karsh. Grey Owl's wife, Anahareo, was not so welcoming, however. After trying to strangle the already broken man, she left him for good. Weeks later, while visiting Montreal, Grey Owl married again. On his marriage licence he gave his name as Archie McNeil, adopting the name of his fictional father. Perhaps he'd begun to believe his own lies. His bride, Yvonne Perrier, could not have known what an unwise choice she had made.

Back in England, the name of the exotic and compelling Grey Owl was still on everyone's lips. Two little girls in

London, Elizabeth and Margaret by name, were especially anxious to meet him, and so their father, King George VI, made the necessary arrangements. Grey Owl's health was almost completely depleted by now, but he still insisted on protecting his false majesty. When he heard that he and other honoured guests were to wait in a reception hall for the royal family to make their entrance, he quickly made some arrangements of his own. King George, Queen Elizabeth and the princesses would await *his* entrance into the hall at Buckingham Palace, and that was exactly what happened. The command performance was a great success and was followed by 130 public lectures in the British Isles.

With Yvonne, his fifth wife, still by his side, Grey Owl sailed back to North America, where he launched into yet another lecture tour, all the while subsisting on raw eggs and whisky. By the time he finally returned to his home in Saskatchewan, his life, which had largely been a lie, was almost over. He died on April 13, 1938.

Radio stations and newspapers throughout North America and England were quick to report his death. One of the people most interested in the news was Grey Owl's first wife, Angele. She had been following his career with great interest. She was also well aware of his actual family background, and as a result, it only took a few hours for the truth about his identity to surface.

It was difficult for people to accept that this man whom they'd so admired had duped them. Many of them refused to believe that Archie Belaney/Grey Owl had perpetrated such a successful hoax. Grey Owl's publisher, Lovat Dickson, believed in his author's story so completely that it took 40 years for Dickson to realize he'd been conned.

To this day, there are many biographies of Grey Owl that studiously omit any references to his numerous marriages, his irresponsible behaviour toward the children he fathered or his excessive drinking, to say nothing of his fraudulent identity. Perhaps those writers feel that the efforts he put into raising society's appreciation for nature outweigh the enormous deception he committed. Without question, Archibald Stansfeld Belaney masterminded and executed one of the most widely accepted hoaxes of the 20th century.

Long Lance

In 1919, a dashing young man presented himself at the offices of the *Calgary Herald*. He wanted to work for the newspaper as a reporter, he said, specializing in "Indian issues." According to his application, the man was a full-blooded Cherokee who had fought with the Canadian Expeditionary Force in the First World War and was a graduate of West Point Academy. The *Herald* hired him immediately, feeling that having a journalist like Long Lance associated with the organization would be a real advantage.

Long Lance's profile in the community soon rose as he worked tirelessly for Native rights. He was frequently invited to soirees where he often gave the after-dinner address. A shoe company sought him to endorse their products, which he did. He even became a movie star. The film *Silent Enemy* drew attention to the plight of Canada's Natives in the Far North. In recognition of his efforts, the Blackfoot ceremonially welcomed him to their nation and bestowed upon him the honorary name Buffalo Child.

In 1927, at the age of 37, Long Lance wrote his autobiography, detailing a poverty-stricken childhood as a Blackfoot in Montana. His fame grew. As his exposure broadened, so did the attention to Natives' causes—until the people he grew up with recognized him as one of their own.

This man was not Chief Buffalo Child Long Lance, a Cherokee graduate of West Point or a Blackfoot from Montana, but Sylvester Clark Long, the grandson of African-American slaves who believed they also had white and Cherokee ancestry. Long had apparently applied for admission to West Point, but his application had been rejected. He had served adequately in the Canadian Forces during the First World War, but he certainly had never received any of the commendations that he claimed.

Sylvester Clark Long, alias Chief Buffalo Child Long Lance, was devastated at being found out and losing the life he'd come to love. In March of 1932 he took his own life.

Although the similarities between Grey Owl and Long Lance are remarkable, somehow Long Lance seems more admirable. He came from a deeply deprived background and fought for the rights of other oppressed people, unlike

Grey Owl, who posed as a member of another culture because he found his own background less than exciting. However, both men used their disguises to fight successfully for those who needed protection. Few hoaxes accomplish anything even close to being so beneficial.

Will James

While the story of Long Lance is considerably less well known than that of Grey Owl, remarkably, there is yet a third very similar imposter from that same era.

Cowboy artist and writer Will James began life in Montana, born under a wagon. Sadly, and perhaps not too surprisingly considering those conditions, James' mother died giving birth to him. Just a few years later, his father also died, leaving the boy in the care of a kindly family friend, a French-Canadian trapper known as Bopy.

For years, the orphan was never far from Bopy's side. During the Canadian winters, the older man taught Will to trap and hunt. During the summers, the two would travel to various ranches in Montana, where they worked as cowboys. Over the years, Bopy nurtured in young Will the skills he would need for the life ahead of him. Then tragedy struck: Bopy drowned in the frigid Red Deer River, leaving Will James, then in his late teens, utterly alone in the world.

There was little else for the youngster to do but to continue living the only life he'd ever known. One summer, Will tried to add cattle rustling to his skill set, but the attempt wasn't really successful. As a matter of fact, it cost him 15 months in a Nevada prison. Shortly after his prison stay, he signed on for a short stint in the US Army.

Next, Will joined a Wild West show, where he rode bucking broncos and sold his artwork—full-colour drawings of the western landscape and cowboy life. His pictures proved to be so popular that he began selling them to magazines.

By the early 1920s, the once-lonely cowboy had married a teenager named Alice Conradt and had also established himself as a regular paid contributor to popular magazines, supplementing his pictures with articles about the Wild West. His personal knowledge of the life he depicted in his stories and pictures made him extremely popular with the magazines' readers. It seemed that Will James had found his niche because, despite his idiosyncratic and ungrammatical writing style, his work was hailed by critics. He wrote and published an astonishing 24 books between 1924 and 1942.

James also worked in Hollywood, where his skills as a rider not only earned him numerous roles as a movie stuntman but also made film producers aware of his literary achievements. As a result, many of his books were made into movies, including *Smoky the Cowhorse*, which had won the prestigious Newbery Award.

There's no doubt that Will James led a successful life. The trouble is, it was all a lie. Will James, born under a wagon in Montana, never existed. The man who became Will James was actually Joseph Ernest Nephtali Dufault, born into a large French-Canadian family in Saint-Nazaire-d'Acton, Quebec, in 1892. Interestingly, one of the few factual pieces of information about the imposter Will James was his close association with a man whose name at least sounded like "Bopy." According to historical documents, it's likely that a man named Beaupré befriended the teenager and taught him many of the skills he'd need as a trapper and a cowhand.

In his fictionalized autobiography, *Lone Cowboy*, published in 1930, Joseph Dufault/Will James credited his friendship with Beaupré/Bopy for the French-Canadian flavour in his speech, just as Grey Owl had credited his non-Native father with the genes that gave him his blue eyes. Ironically, the announcer for the first Wild West show James ever worked billed him as "Bullshit Bill."

Sadly, like Grey Owl and Long Lance before him, the constant stress of living a life of deception took its toll on the man who had become Will James. He drank heavily, and by 1936 his wife had left him and creditors had foreclosed on his ranch. In 1942, the cowboy from Quebec died in poverty, an event that went all but unnoticed at the time. But in the years since, his art has gained a considerable following and is now highly prized by collectors.

The Great Imposter

On March 13, 1951, a man walked into the Royal Canadian Navy's recruiting office in Saint John, New Brunswick, and announced, "I am Dr. Joseph Cyr of this province and I feel it is my duty, now that we are again in war, to volunteer my services where they can be of most help."

Considering the difficulty the navy was having attracting physicians during the Korean War years, an unsolicited volunteer was an unusual enough situation, but what makes the case even more interesting is that this man could also have introduced himself as Jefferson Baird Thorne, Martin Godgart, Frank Kingston, Ferdinand Waldo Demara Jr., Fred W. Demara, Dr. Robert Linton French, Brother John Payne, Dr. Cecil Boyce Hamann or Ben W. Jones because, amazingly, he had documentation verifying every one of those identities—and more. Dr. Joseph Cyr was just the current alias in a long list of alter egos perpetrated by a pudgy, rather nondescript man who hadn't yet turned 30 years of age.

By sundown that day, the man had been flown to Ottawa, where he passed inspection by the medical officer selection board. He later recalled that the men questioning him only seemed concerned that he might be the type of physician with a yen toward experimental medicine, and they didn't want Canada's sailors used as guinea pigs. The man pretending to be Dr. Cyr had little trouble convincing the committee that he was an acceptably traditional practitioner, and within a few days he was posted to the naval hospital in Halifax as a lieutenant.

Considering that "Dr. Joseph Cyr" was really Ferdinand Waldo Demara Jr., a man who'd never had more than rudimentary first-aid training, it would be reasonable to assume that he'd be extremely nervous—and he may have been—but given the long list of aliases already to his credit, it was obvious there was nothing ordinary about this man. What he lacked in medical training he made up for in nerve.

Cyr approached one of the hospital's supervising doctors with a request supposedly from lumberjacks who were working in northern camps and isolated from proper medical treatment. These men, he maintained, had asked for a booklet that would cover the treatment of the most common illnesses and injuries. He added that it would be best if the information could be written in a way that would be easy for a layman to understand.

Two days later, "Dr. Cyr" had a basic medical guide in his possession. The hastily prepared information was comprehensive enough that it proved useful throughout his entire career as a doctor in the Royal Canadian Navy.

Cyr may have been a fraud, but he wasn't an unfeeling man. He didn't want anyone to suffer because of his ruse, and as a result, he developed a reputation as a man who was always willing to discuss a diagnosis with a fellow doctor. Then, no matter what the other doctor recommended, Cyr always took the advice.

Unfortunately, just as the quack was becoming comfortable in the hospital setting, the navy posted him to a ship—a very large aircraft carrier. Of course, the medical fraternity that had unwittingly covered for Cyr in the hospital didn't exist on board HMCS *Magnificent*. There was only his superior, the commanding medical officer, and it didn't take very long for this officer to become disillusioned with the lieutenant's diagnostic skills, or more correctly, his lack of diagnostic skills. But again the imposter found a solution. If he was unsure about a patient's treatment, he simply hid the man in out-of-the-way quarters and posted a quarantine sign while he desperately read through medical texts in the hopes of finding a cure.

Cyr's system worked well enough that no one died, and so when *Magnificent* was temporarily docked in Halifax, he treated himself to a day out on the town, during which he met a lovely young lady named Catherine. She clearly thought the young medical officer was fine husband material and immediately set about planning for their wedding, which would take place in Montreal.

Cyr dutifully boarded a westbound train from Halifax, but oddly, considering all the subterfuge he'd managed to that point in his life, the sight of his beloved and her family waiting for him was too much. He fled from the train as it eased into the station at Montreal and hid in the bushes until he thought it would be safe to climb on board again. His calculations were badly off, however, because Catherine was on the train waiting for him. They rode together to Winnipeg, where she realized that he loved his country more than he loved her, and she flew back to Halifax.

Alone again, Cyr continued westbound to Vancouver, where he transferred to a ferry bound for Vancouver Island.

At his new posting at Esquimalt he was assigned to the destroyer HMCS *Cayuga* as the ship's medical officer.

Naively, *Cayuga*'s captain, Commander James Plomer, was deeply relieved to see Dr. Cyr, for he'd been suffering with a severe toothache that needed immediate attention. The imposter needed to buy himself some time to determine if there was a supply of Novocaine on the ship and then, if there was, to figure out how to administer it. Worse, he wasn't even sure he'd be able to tell which tooth needed to be pulled.

The Great Imposter was strictly alone, backed only by his own audacity. Once again that was apparently all he needed. Less than an hour later, the captain was pain free and recovering from a successful dental procedure. Dr. Joseph Cyr's time aboard *Cayuga* was off to a promising start. That must have been a relief, albeit temporary, because there were harrowing days ahead.

Although he was popular with his shipmates, he could, of course, never be open or honest with anyone. To add to that stress, they were sailing into the North Korean battlefront. Cyr's worst fears were realized when they pulled alongside a small Korean ship laden with badly injured men. Cries of "Get Dr. Cyr! Get Dr. Cyr!" echoed through *Cayuga*.

What Cyr found would have challenged even a well-trained medical practitioner. Sixteen men were badly injured and an additional three were in such critical condition that he feared they would die if not attended to quickly—by a skilled surgeon. The situation became even more dangerous when a storm hit the area. There was indeed rough sailing ahead for *Cayuga*.

As the ship rode increasingly strong swells, the crew set up a makeshift operating room. Cyr chose to work first on the man he thought was most seriously injured. He injected the patient with sodium pentothal, but the solution wasn't strong enough to sedate the man. Cyr added a face mask full of ether before taking a scalpel and cutting an incision across the man's chest. Moments later he removed a bullet lodged in the pericardium—the sac surrounding the heart— and then crudely stitched the incision closed.

But Cyr's work was far from finished; two more men required surgery. He removed shrapnel from the next patient's groin and a piece of rib from the third man's lung.

He had begun the first surgeries in the evening. By the time he finished, it was morning, and Cyr was exhausted. He helped himself to a liberal dose of the ship's rum before collapsing on his bunk and sleeping soundly for the entire day. When he awakened, the men he'd operated on were back on their own ship.

Word of Dr. Cyr's heroics reached the press, and within days a complete report of the skilled and courageous surgeon's accomplishments in a jerry-rigged operating room on the high seas ran in every Canadian daily newspaper. As if that weren't bad enough, Ferdinand Demara, alias Joseph Cyr, MD, appeared to believe his own publicity.

A few days later, the impersonator asked to take the

ship's boat to the Korean port where his surgical patients were resting. He was shocked by the filth and squalor that he found and ordered that the area be given a thorough cleaning. He also began treating other sick and injured.

It didn't take long for people in neighbouring villages to learn that there was a doctor nearby. Soon the sick and injured were streaming in to see him. One of the procedures he performed even rated a write-up in the prestigious medical periodical *The Lancet*.

Of course a story this full of human interest drew attention, and the real Dr. Joseph Cyr, who was innocently practising medicine in Edmundston, New Brunswick, began to be harassed by reporters. He acknowledged the coincidence of the name, but assured the journalists that he was not the man they were interested in. Then a newspaper published a photograph of the man who'd performed surgery aboard *Cayuga*. The real Dr. Cyr was shocked to realize that his identity had been stolen—by a man he knew as Brother John Payne. Local newspapers ran with the revelation. The navy and the public all learned the truth from those reports.

On board *Cayuga*, Commander Plomer, whose infected tooth the poser had extracted, suspended the man from duty and confined him to quarters. Cyr/Demara responded by raiding the ship's stores of rum until he was all but comatose and suffering from alcohol poisoning. He was arrested and escorted back to Esquimalt where, ever the imposter, he produced credentials certifying that he was actually Dr. Cecil B. Hamann. It didn't take long for the navy to follow "Hamann's" paper trail back to Fred W. Demara who, of course, was Ferdinand Waldo Demara Jr. and had absolutely no medical qualifications.

On November 21, 1951, the Royal Canadian Navy issued a one-sentence press release: "Ferdinand Waldo Demara, alias Cyr, will be discharged from the naval service at Esquimalt today." They did not lay charges.

Demara returned to the United States and continued his truly extraordinary life. He worked as a chaplain in the Los Angeles area, where he befriended a variety of interesting people, some of them very well known. In his capacity as a chaplain, he administered last rites to actor Steve McQueen.

Demara died from complications of diabetes in June 1982. He was 61 years old and had, by anyone's definition, lived an incredible hoax-filled life.

CHAPTER

4

Spiritualism

Keeping Their Spirits Up

During the mid-to-late 1800s and into the early years of the 20th century, scientific discoveries were shaking the comfortable, myth-based world that people had enjoyed for centuries. The very foundation of society's long-held belief system— religion—was being challenged by Charles Darwin, author of *The Origin of Species*, and his disciples.

Worse, people were surrounded by death. Previously healthy young women routinely died in childbirth. A family's breadwinner might die from an infection, just days after cutting his or her finger at work. These tragedies, or even just the possibility of such seemingly arbitrary catastrophes, were devastating. It's no wonder that people were obsessed with death and created elaborate mourning rituals. Those who were grieving needed some process with which to comfort themselves. Enter the Victorian era's spiritualism movement and its associated hucksters.

A career as a psychic medium suddenly became appealing for those with a strong inclination for fast money and an equally strong disregard for people's suffering. It was a perfect context for sophisticated (and some not-so-sophisticated) hoaxes. Fortunately, the movement also led to the emergence of skeptical investigators with a more questioning bent. Even so, it's a testimony to the popularity of popular mediums and seances that when a fraudster was caught, it was big news.

On October 24, 1879, Victoria's *Daily Colonist* reported that George W. Tomes, a resident of that city's Broadway Avenue, took his out-of-town friend F.A. Tremaine to a spiritualist seance being held "up town." The article states that, "The two friends went to . . . a well-furnished, brownstone house. They were met at the door by an old man who, after consulting a memorandum book to see if the seats were all taken, admitted them on payment of $1.00 each."

The seance was held in the "back parlor" of the house that, not surprisingly, was poorly lit. There were "three rows of chairs and about fifty people . . . of whom four or five were women." Tomes and Tremaine also apparently noted that there was "a small cabinet fixed against the wall." Carpenters must have earned a good living during the spiritualist era because such cabinets were mainstays of psychic hoaxers. The newspaper report specified, "The greater part of the front of the cabinet was concealed by a curtain, but there was room at one side for a small window."

As the seance began, "the old man who had acted as treasurer announced that the medium and her company would not be responsible for manifestations of the spirits and he then requested that the audience sing some familiar air, such as The Sweet By-and-By." Shortly after this, the seance began and "the medium, a stout woman, entered the cabinet and immediately afterwards a hand was shown at the window and a foot at the bottom of the curtain."

Next, a little boy who was referred to as "Jimmy the Newsboy" stepped from the cabinet into the room and began to dance. With all the singing and now the dancing too, clearly this was to be an evening of entertainment, if nothing else.

By now, Tomes and Tremaine had apparently both seen and heard as much as they could stomach. The pair decided to "seize the next spirit that should appear." Then "there was a loud knocking," and a disembodied voice asked if the audience would like to see a spirit. Of course, the crowd answered with a resounding "yes," but before the two skeptics had time to react, the group was told that "the spirits were confused" and only wanted to communicate with one particular person—the person who had recently "had a conversation with the spirit who was familiarly called Mary."

The article went on to indicate that "the subsequent proceedings are best described in Mr. Tomes' language" and followed with a very long and intriguing quote from Tomes:

> I moved toward the old man who admitted me, and who was standing at the far end of the room. He told me I had better take my seat; but I said I'd stay where I was. He repeated his admonition and I went to the room and stood in front of a woman. The spirit Mary then came out into the room about eight feet from the cabinet. The passage was clear in front of me, and I went for her like a streak of lightning and threw my arms around her. She screamed and struggled and several of the men ran to her assistance. My friend ran to help me but he fell over the seats and the spirit got away from me. That ghost weighed 150 pounds if she weighed an ounce, and I fully identified her as the medium.

It looked like the medium's gig was all but up. Then Tomes added, "The woman who had been sitting behind where I'd been standing cried out, 'You nearly killed my daughter and you ought to be shot with a pistol and I've a good mind to shoot you for threatening a spirit that way.'"

Not dismayed by the apparent threat against his life, Tomes noted, "The spirit had very little clothing on and her face was whitened to give her a ghostly look."

At that point, the evening's entertainment was clearly over, and both "the believers and the unbelievers were dismissed." After all that publicity in the local newspaper, it's likely that the psychic scammers were forced to pick up stakes in Victoria and move on.

Across the country, the *Ottawa Daily Free Press* reported on December 17, 1895, that boys in "a certain public institution" had perpetrated a considerably less sophisticated hoax by covering themselves in "white sheets and while thus garbed visited several adjoining rooms, all while emitting low gutteral [*sic*] sounds that gave a canny suggestion of another world."

In the colourful language of that day, the unnamed journalist declared, "Naturally those visited were much disturbed and gave expression to their fear in loud shouts. One of those whose slumbers was disturbed was so overcome with fear that he was unable to move from his bed and confined his efforts to muttering prayers that he might be saved from a sudden and awful fate." A few others, however, apparently decided to show the boys that such hoaxes were not appreciated. "Two of those who were made the victims of the joke secured small hatchets and went in search of the marauders whom they succeeded in running to earth after some difficulty."

The publication of such a detailed article about what was essentially a childish practical joke indicates how deeply Canadian culture was immersed in spiritualism. This phenomenon continued into the 20th century, as proven by an article carried in the *Brantford Courier* on October 19, 1907. Interestingly, especially considering the era, the headline read: THE GHOST WAS ARRESTED WITH VERY LITTLE ON.

The body of the article clearly reveals that there were well-divided camps in this spiritualist movement: the believers, the skeptics and those who clearly had fun reporting the controversial events. It's worthy of note that a cabinet is again involved in the hoax. The article states, "A raid on a spiritualist meeting last night at 572 Bathurst Street [Toronto] furnished some lively scenes and ended in a free fight and the capture of a ghost."

This raid was accomplished very cleverly by policemen posing as believers in the abilities of the medium, but even so, the psychics were apparently suspicious of these undercover officers, for the *Courier*'s reporter noted, "Some difficulty was experienced by the officers in getting in as, in addition to the payment of a dollar the visitors to the séances are closely scrutinized and are liable to be refused admission."

Despite the "difficulty," officers Brisbane and Hogue were able to join the audience and determined that "the ghost turned out to be Rev. Elizabeth Howland, an American lady of some 34 years of age."

The two police officers bided their time as "the Howland woman went into a cabinet and divested herself of clothing to the satisfaction of a jury of ladies. After the lights were turned out, a number of so-called spirit materializations were performed, and members of the audience who had given their names to Mrs. Howland at a previous meeting were called forward to receive messages from dead friends."

In addition, a man named P.C. Hogue from Hamilton was visited by "one of his dead friends," who oddly assured him that his business "deal would go through and that it would turn out to be very profitable for him."

At that point, the party apparently became rowdy and something of a melee broke out:

> When the spirit of a child called [out to] Mrs. Lowe she went forward and a moment after she thrust her hand into the cabinet and dragged out a spirit after which great confusion prevailed . . . A burly woman in the audience dragged Mrs. Lowe back by the hair while Constable Brisbane seized hold of the male prisoner [Rev. Clarence Howland] who was advancing to the assistance of his partner in life.
>
> Brisbane turned on his electric torch and called out that they were police officers. He was immediately borne down on by a number of men who flung themselves on him and in the fracas his torch went out. The officer got to his feet and grabbed his billy and fought the crowd: he had one big man hors de combat when the scuffle was over.
>
> In the meantime the other constable had seized the female prisoner and at once became the storm centre again.

But the officer was clearly also a gentleman because when he saw that she was nearly naked, "he placed her again in the cabinet from which she emerged in a short time better clothed." Whew—propriety was preserved.

"The prisoners and their cabinet and part of the spirit clothing were conveyed to No. 3 [police] station where both prisoners were charged with fraud being released shortly after midnight on bail.

"They were attended by an excited group of followers." No doubt!

A couple of years before this rousing incident, on Tuesday, November 7, 1905, the *Sherbrooke Daily Record* ran an article about a local man, Arthur T. Neate, who rallied a few of his like-minded friends to join him at a meeting held in "the headquarters of the Spiritualists." It should be no surprise by now to learn that a cabinet was prominently displayed at the front of the room where the session was to be held.

Neate revealed that he had covertly carried an "electric pocket lamp" (presumably what we would today call a flashlight) with him, and that the session "opened with prayer and hymns." The lights were turned down, and while the crowd sang, the medium opened the cabinet door and stepped inside. Shortly, "a white-robed form appeared from the cabinet into which the medium had retired."

Now, the skeptical Mr. Neate was a quick study. He shone his "electric pocket lamp" while one of his accomplices "turned up the gas." Mr. Neate then "seized hold of the form that emerged from the cabinet and, although the figure was wearing a false moustache its identity as the medium was plain."

Neate had the scoundrel dead to rights, or as the article read, "the exposure caused great indignation. The medium was found dressed up as a spirit form, much to the horror and disgust of the sitters." But all's well that ends well because the newspaper concluded their account by noting that "the money that had been paid" to the hoaxers by those in attendance was returned.

Mr. Neate was pleased with the results and suggested, "This incident might prevent others from being duped." Clearly, his work there was done.

But just because there were hoaxes galore within the field, does that mean that spiritualism itself was a hoax? If that were so, then why did so many well-educated and well-known people attend private seances, known as "home circles," where no one stood to profit from anything that did or did not occur during them? Some very prominent folks including Canada's prime minister William Lyon Mackenzie King and author Sir Arthur Conan Doyle took part in these sessions.

Other devotees of spiritualism might not have been as well known internationally but were certainly significant figures within their communities. Dr. Glen Hamilton, a physician, held regular seances at his Winnipeg home, as did Sydenham, Ontario, dentist Samuel Augustus Aykroyd, the great-grandfather of actor Dan Aykroyd. According to the younger Aykroyd's foreword in his father's book *A History of Ghosts*, the campy 1980s movie *Ghostbusters* had roots in the tales handed down from the century before.

Spiritualism and its attendant practitioners, both the ethical ones and those whose morals didn't extend past their profit margin, flourished roughly until the start of the

First World War, when Canadians' attentions were diverted to much more crucial matters. But even today in our scientifically sophisticated era, it's still pretty easy to find someone eager to tell you your fortune. Sadly, the ratio of hoaxers to those with legitimate skills probably hasn't changed over the past 100 to 150 years. Buyer beware!

Dr. Pepper's Lonely Hoax

When advertisements began appearing around Montreal in the early weeks of 1873, it didn't take long for a mood of excited anticipation to take hold. Soon the atmosphere in the city was almost electric with expectation—and it was no wonder. None other than the internationally acclaimed Professor John Henry Pepper, FCS, would soon be visiting the city. What an honour!

The famed Professor Pepper would be performing at the Queen's Hall, a theatre on St. Catherine Street. This was *not* an event to be missed. Audiences in France, Germany, Spain, India, Russia and the United States had all been dazzled by Pepper's supernatural presentation. Now it was Canada's turn.

People went to great lengths to attend the event, even rearranging their schedules if necessary. This was not going to be any ordinary, run-of-the mill seance—far from it. Professor Pepper's apparitions were not just the common garden-variety ghosts so popular in that era. Incredibly, these spirits were officially sanctioned, protected by a patent that was duly registered in the United Kingdom.

Spiritualism

On the night of the performance, those lucky enough to have a ticket eagerly entered the theatre where the stage had been set to resemble a room in a Victorian-era mansion. To enhance the dignity and drama of the occasion, the lighting was muted and drew attention to a lone figure, a young man, sitting at a desk and appearing to be utterly lost in thought.

A moment later, a second figure came into view. The audience drew its collective breath, not because this second figure was a lovely young woman dressed in a long, hooded robe but because she was transparent!

Those gathered whispered among themselves; some stood up in horror and fascination. Of course they'd heard that Pepper would demonstrate that the dead actually did walk among the living, but none had ever seen it before. How could they not believe what was right there before their eyes? As this hooded woman made her way across the boards, she walked in front of furniture and windows, and yet those objects were visible all the time. The audience could see right through her. She was a ghost.

But, of course, like so many others in that era, Pepper's show was a hoax, although not in the manner you might think. John Henry Pepper was, in fact, very candid about how he created his ghost. It was nothing more than a trick with reflected light. He was a scientist, not a psychic, and he wasn't trying to fool anyone. Quite the contrary, he was trying to explain to the naive masses just how such illusions were performed.

But if Pepper wasn't trying to mislead anyone, his employers didn't share his integrity. In fact *they* were the swindlers. Polytechnic Joint Stock Company in London, England, the group that produced the show, collected 12,000 pounds during the initial year's run. From that amount, the poor, gullible, honest Pepper was paid a miserly 200 pounds. The original hoax may have been on him, but the scientist's name has lived on. Even today, magicians all over the world respect the elegance and physics of the trick of light known as Pepper's Ghost.

Picture This

Closely related to the topic of spiritualism is the field of spirit photography—a practice that has enjoyed a resurgence of interest with today's digital cameras.

Photography was in its infancy when the spiritualism movement began in the mid-1800s. The first "ghost" photo no doubt occurred accidentally when a camera's glass plates weren't cleaned of silver bromide gel before being re-used. This would create a residual, indistinct image from the previous photograph on the next one taken.

Even 50 years later, taking a photograph was still a complicated procedure, one that was time-consuming enough to offer plenty of opportunities for tinkering at different stages of the process until the desired effect had been created. Add to this people's fascination with the possibility that there is some sort of life after death, and quicker than you can say trick photography, along came those anxious to learn that trade!

Most spirit photos can be proven to be fakes, but a few ghostly images have defied rational explanation despite having been investigated many times. The picture of the "Brown Lady of Raynham Hall," for instance, is commonly accepted as being genuine even though it was taken 210 years after the subject's death! The cause of Lady Dorothy Townshend's untimely death in 1726 was contentious. Some say she died of smallpox, others think her broken heart simply stopped beating, while a third group believes she fell down the staircase at her home at Raynham Hall in Norfolk. And that staircase is exactly where her ghost has been photographed. When the magazine *Country Life* ran a photo of the palatial staircase at the manor in 1936, readers were shocked to see the slightly see-through image of the estate's previous occupant. This picture has held up to professional scrutiny for more than 70 years.

Perhaps by coincidence, perhaps not, another world-famous spirit photograph that has equally withstood the test of time and professional investigation was also taken in an old English house. The photo of the Greenwich Ghost was taken in 1966, at Queen's House, Greenwich. The unlikely photographer was Reverend R.W. Hardy. The picture has been described as showing "a shrouded figure" hunched over beside a staircase. The print and the negative it was made from have been examined—even by the film manufacturer, Kodak—but to date no one has suggested how the photo could have been faked.

Photographers skilled in creating multiple-exposure images, such as this one, were in great demand and made a good, if immoral, living. LIBRARY OF CONGRESS 3G01845

Of course, not all pictures of ghosts would hold up to such examination, as witnessed by this rather light-hearted article in the Saturday, December 21, 1901, edition of the *Toronto Empire and News*. Even the headline might have been written with a bit of humour in mind, as it stated: SPIRIT PICTURE FAKE EXPOSED.

It seemed that Toronto police staff inspector Archibald "and his men" arrested Ezra Glassco and a woman named Mrs. Love. Then the article helpfully provided a detailed description of how to produce "spirit pictures."

The process was described as being "chiefly remarkable for the astounding effect it produces upon the audience." The unnamed journalist continues:

> There is shown to the audience a seemingly perfectly blank sheet of light canvas. This canvas is placed on an easel, both sides of the canvas having been first shown to be blank. A lamp is then placed several feet behind the easel, rendering the canvas transparent and showing that it is impossible for any one to touch the canvas from behind without being seen. The lights in the room are then lowered a little, leaving the room in sort of a twilight in which nevertheless, everything is plainly visible. A piano then contributes a little music or the audience is asked to sing hymns. While they are singing a "spirit" picture is slowly precipitated upon the cloth in colors, in full view of the audience assembled. The impression left upon the minds of the audience is, of course, that "spirit" hands are at work in their midst.

All of this is conveniently located adjacent to a cabinet. The reporter then continues on in his description and reveals the trickery:

> The secret is that the canvas is prepared beforehand as follows: Suppose you wish to produce a picture in blue, yellow and brown colors. Procure from your druggist a little sulphate of iron for blue, nitrate of bismuth for yellow and sulphate of copper for brown. Dissolve these separately in a little warm water and your "colors" are ready. Take three separate brushes, a brush for each color, and paint a picture, landscape, portrait, or whatever you wish to appear upon the canvas or upon a screen of unbleached muslin. Muslin is best. When the "colors" are dry, they are invisible and the muslin does not look as if it had been touched. Now, when you are ready to give your performance, set the screen on an easel in front of the cabinet upon the stage, of course, from which you or your assistant can put the finishing touches upon the picture, unseen by the audience.

Then, under the sub-headline BRINGING OUT THE PICTURE, the writer continues:

> Get some prussiate of potash from your druggist and put it in a bottle atomizer. Let the canvas be slightly dampened with a cloth wet with cold water, and when the music begins, your assistant in the cabinet takes the atomizer and from behind sprays all over the back of the screen with the solution of prussiate potash, which slowly brings the colors out. For the dampening of the cloth with cold water some excuse may sometimes be necessary, for instance, it may be claimed that the sensitiveness

of the spirit influence is thus increased. If it is practicable to dampen the cloth without the knowledge of the audience the trick is a little more impressive.

The effect is weird in the extreme. The music covers the sound of the atomizer. The audience can see by means of the light at back that no one approaches the screen and, of course, they believe that they are in the presence of a "spirit" picture.

In closing, the document states, "This is a feat performed by but few mediums, as few know the secret. Those who do know it are reaping a golden harvest."

Well, perhaps they did until that story ran in the newspaper anyway. Presumably it would have been wise to visit a number of different drugstores in order to acquire all the needed supplies without making any one "druggist" suspicious about what you were up to.

Photos taken with today's digital cameras can include a phenomenon known as orbs: white disks that seem to float about the scene that has been photographed. Some of these orbs are transparent, while others appear to be solid. Some orbs even look as though there are images of faces within them. Scientists have declared that these strange little anomalies can also show up using a camera that requires film, but that they are much more likely to be captured with a digital camera. The bad news for a photo-hoaxer–wannabe is that whether or not an orb shows up in a picture doesn't seem to be something anyone can control—yet.

5

Out of This World

Alien Invasion

Even today, the residential community of Oak Bay, in the Greater Victoria area of Vancouver Island, is as peaceful and calm a community as you'd find anywhere in Canada. Imagine then what a sleepy little place it must have been 60 years ago. No wonder the local police were surprised on Saturday, September 6, 1952, when they received a phone call from Oak Bay resident Cowper Adams informing them, "There's a spaceship in my backyard."

Probably more amused than concerned, the police dispatcher dutifully responded by sending an officer in a patrol car to check into the situation. That officer was soon phoning back into headquarters with the report that not only was there a spaceship in a backyard but that humanoid beings in "strange uniforms were issuing from it and running around."

The news spread quickly as nearby residents noticed the alien invasion and phoned local radio stations and newspapers. "Reporters and more police came running. Oak Bay was in a lather," according to an article in the September 8, 1952, edition of the *Edmonton Journal*.

Once the details of this strange event began to emerge, the police confirmed that the extraterrestrial vehicle was not, in fact, from a universe far beyond our own, but that it had been built locally—very locally—in the Oak Bay back-yard where it currently stood. The "spaceship" was made of aluminum and plastic and wasn't designed for intergalac-tic travel at all but rather was merely a prop for a costume party. The men in "strange uniforms" were guests Adams had invited to his "space happy" costume party.

It took several hours for the neighbourhood to settle down. Once cooler heads prevailed, the police went back to their police station, the reporters went back to their news-paper and radio offices, and the uniformed space men went back to their party.

It seems unlikely that police today would be as under-standing if they were called out to investigate a hoax by the person who was responsible for perpetrating it in the first place.

Radio Silence

On Thursday, October 25, 1956, the *Calgary Herald* carried some especially intriguing news under a headline that read, A VOICE FROM MARS ON NOV. 7? The article, written by a journalist named John Taylor, opened with words that were practically guaranteed to grab the readers' attention: "A two-minute message broadcast direct from a flying saucer by Martians may be aired over [radio station] CFAC on November 7 at 11:30 p.m."

Before offering the explanation for such an amazing statement, Mr. Taylor reminded skeptics that "the existence of Martians and flying saucers has not been proved or disproved."

The logistics of this history-making broadcast were to be straightforward. Calgary radio station CFAC would "discontinue its evening program for two minutes on Nov. 7 but still leave its carrier signal on the air to stand by for the message from Mars." This message would be broadcast "from a spaceship which will be at an altitude of 10,000 feet over Los Angeles. This ship will be visible to all the people as it will be illuminated by a [Martian] force field."

Where could reporter Taylor have obtained this information, to say nothing of the assurance that the facts were correct? After all, the *Herald* was (and still is) a reliable, respectable newspaper, and its readers weren't accustomed to seeing unsubstantiated, tabloid-like stories in its pages. Well, it seems that the source of Taylor's facts was none other than the Martians themselves, who "notified earth of its forthcoming broadcast several months ago."

Presumably to avoid any language barrier, that earlier message was sent telepathically and recorded here on earth. Obviously, understanding its meaning wasn't an issue because newspapers, radio stations and other interested parties were soon all privy to the information from outer space. Ben Metcalf, a reporter from the *Province* in Vancouver, confirmed that he had heard the tape recording, and he asserted, "There is no indication here that it is a commercial gag."

Then, possibly in an attempt to prove the authenticity of the claim, CFAC declared that they intended to air a portion of the transmission that evening at 10:15. The radio station's manager, Bert Cairns, promised Calgarians that the complete communication would be heard "at a later date." In the meantime, it was recommended that people prepare themselves for this intergalactic event so that they "may obtain an insight into the thoughts of a Martian." Listeners were also told that even though "Calgary will not be fortunate enough to have the flying saucer over the city, CFAC with its modern equipment, will pick up the message."

In order to assure everyone that these weren't last-minute arrangements, *Herald* readers were advised that this "appointment between Martian and man" had been made "several months ago."

Members of a flying saucer club in Vancouver had also

heard this fascinating audiotape. They maintained that they'd received it from a like-minded club in California. A Vancouver representative of the club named Anderson, who lived on 8th Avenue West in that city, revealed that "the voice on the tape was that of a Californian whose brain process translated the message into English."

The Martian politely identified himself by title and name—a name that the *Calgary Herald* newspaper spelled Mon-ka—and indicated that he was a "Martian councillor from space." The Martian advised the Californian that he was "speaking from his radio station KOR 'on the planet which you call Mars.'" During his three-minute message, Mon-ka explained that "his government had not been in a position to communicate with world leaders and its governments prior to 1956."

Mon-ka went on to telepathically transmit assurances that would "dispel any arguments that life on Mars did not exist," and he seemed to be well aware of the human tendency toward aggression. "We do not advise your military to attempt to hinder or to force us down for this would bring disaster to them. We will do nothing but speak from our craft," Mon-ka assured humankind, before adding the slightly ominous comment "People of the Earth, it is time you knew the truth."

In the meantime, it seemed that all the Earthlings could do was wait. But rather than waste the entire two weeks, the *Herald* ran a contest for children in the Calgary area, asking them to submit drawings of how they thought the visitor from Mars might look. The best one would win $25, "winner take all."

After only a few days, however, it became apparent that those guidelines would have to be changed because management at the *Herald* hadn't been prepared for the enormous number of entries they received—over 300. In the end, the contest judges combined their two favourite drawings (the body of one and the head of another) for a composite and awarded each of those two artists $12.50. Then, in recognition of other imaginative pictures, the judges also awarded a $10 second prize, a $7.50 third prize and a $5 fourth prize. Special mention was also made of the youngest artist—a three-year-old.

Fortunately, the winners had been chosen by the night of the broadcast because by then, all minds were on alien visitors. An array of UFOs were spotted in the skies over Calgary, and radar in California also detected numerous oddities, including, as promised, a spaceship hovering above Los Angeles at an estimated altitude of 10,000 feet.

Many radio stations throughout Canada and the United States joined CFAC in Calgary and KATY in California's San Luis Obispo in the two minutes of silence at 11:30 P.M.

The radio waves may have been quiet, but the stations' switchboards were certainly not. Calls from concerned citizens flooded the radio stations' phone lines and "unusual" but unspecified "radio activity" was reported. In Calgary,

there was also said to have been a sudden rise in tempera-
ture "to 40 degrees Fahrenheit [5 degrees Celsius]" although
it wasn't reported how much of a rise that was.

According to an article in the *Herald* the next day, "It
was a tense and thrilling two minutes." Disappointingly,
but perhaps not surprisingly, no message from Mars or anywhere else was heard.

Calgary-based paranormal researcher W. Ritchie Benedict
has compiled considerable information about this story and
concludes that "this has always been considered to be a hoax
but, to this day, no one is sure."

It's interesting to note that if you transpose the two
syllables in the Martian's name Mon-ka, you get Ka-Mon,
presumably pronounced "come on," as in "come on folks,
this couldn't possibly be true."

A Circular Debate

Timing can be a crucial factor in determining how successful a particular project will become. In the 1970s, when
the New Age movement was gaining popularity, a growing
number of people began whispering to one another about
the possibility that extraterrestrial travellers had repeatedly
visited the Earth. In 1966, a circular area of flattened ground
was found in Queensland, Australia, and the odd area was
often cited as proof of this possibility. It looked for all the
world as though a flying saucer had landed. How exciting!

A few years later in Southampton, England, two old

friends, Doug Bower and Dave Chorley, were enjoying their regular Friday evening at a local pub when they decided to put a little extra fun and silliness into their lives. Under the cover of darkness, they headed out to a nearby farm. There, equipped with a plank of lumber and a length of rope, they flattened a circle of crops. Quite tickled with their accomplishment, the pair went home to wait and see what reaction there would be to their efforts.

Disappointingly, there was no reaction at all.

Bower and Chorley decided to create a few more crop circles, but those were overlooked too. They moved their efforts to a more visible location. Finally the world took notice. The media, especially British tabloids, were in their glory. Within days, word and photographs of these strange formations had spread all over the world. Everyone was puzzled—everyone, that is, except two quiet, unassuming Englishmen, who were thoroughly gratified that people were admiring their quirky handiwork.

Encouraged, Dave and Doug decided to enlarge the scope of their work. They began making bigger and more intricate patterns, all with their original tool of a piece of lumber tied to a rope.

By now people were doing more than talking; some folks were worrying and others were investigating. Chorley and Bower kept to their routine of meeting each Friday evening at their favourite pub for a quaff or two before heading out on their great circle-making adventure, which, understandably, they were finding considerably more fun than sitting in a smoky tavern for hours at a time.

As with most things in life, the more the two men practised their "craft," the better and faster they became at it, so they began to get more adventuresome with their designs and in the locations they chose. Scientists scrutinized the formations but came away completely stumped, except for one investigator who quite rightly noted that the crop circles only appeared on Saturday mornings. This observation confused everyone even more, except Doug Bower and Dave Chorley, who knew their adventures in cereal artistry only followed their regular evening at the pub. Another scientist pointed out that as the circles always swirled in a clockwise direction they might have been caused by localized whirlwinds. Doug and Dave responded by creating a counter-clockwise pattern.

It seemed that the two men were succeeding in hoaxing the entire world. What fun! But then circles began appearing in places that the two hadn't visited. New Agers took these copycat circles as proof that alien space ships had landed on Earth.

Who knows how long the hoax could have continued had it not been for a small domestic problem in the Bower household. It seems that Mrs. Bower had begun to notice that her husband was getting home very late on Friday nights—actually very early on Saturday mornings—and that he was putting a tremendous number of miles on the car every week. She became suspicious that he was having an affair. In order to save his marriage, Doug had to confess to what he and Dave had been doing on those long Friday-night drives. In 1991, Chorley and Bower took their confession public.

You would expect the world would have been relieved that the mystery was solved, but not so. Many people were angry, and others were embarrassed. The scientists who had been involved were more than a little annoyed to have wasted their time investigating what was effectively a practical joke. For others, these crop circles had become something of a hobby. Some of them enjoyed secretly stamping out increasingly ornate figures, while an even greater number enjoyed investigating them. It turned out that few folks were pleased to hear that the whole thing had been a prank. They retaliated by pointing out that even if the two men had made *some* of the designs, that certainly didn't explain the growing number of crop circles found all over the world.

In Canada, Saskatchewan was the most heavily "circled" area, which makes perfect sense, as that province grows most of the country's cereal crops, but complex crop circles were (and still are) found elsewhere in the country as well, including Alberta, Manitoba, southern Ontario and farms to the east.

Greenpeace created crop circles in western Canada to draw attention to their cause, and on July 1, 2001, near the Port Mann Bridge across British Columbia's Fraser River, crop circles appeared on a hill, accompanied by a roughly produced imitation of the maple leaf as it appears on the Canadian flag. Clearly this instance, timed for Canada Day, was more about patriotism than a possible alien invasion.

Meanwhile, back in England, ground zero for crop circles, a growing number of people were beginning to doubt the validity of Dave Chorley and Doug Bower's claim that they were the culprits. Could their confession itself have been a hoax, or were the men taking credit for something that had a far more complex explanation?

But the circles had to be hoaxes—didn't they?

Unfortunately for those wanting to believe that the phenomenon had been a recent practical joke gone awry, a researcher found a record of a crop circle appearing in southern England in 1880. Proponents of the spaceship theory held this report as proof that these intricate patterns are not the work of hoaxers. Those on the other side of the debate very sensibly pointed out that even in the 1800s there were pranksters.

People in the latter camp might have been interested in a book called *Thirty Indian Legends of Canada*. These traditional Native stories were compiled by Margaret Bemister in the very early 1900s. One story, "The Daughters of the Star," could be of particular interest to devotees of the crop-circle debate. The old legend relates the adventures of White Hawk, a hunter who "came to a circle on the prairie [that] looked as if people had run around in a ring until the grass was trampled down."

What the hunter found especially puzzling was that he "could see no marks of footsteps leading away from the ring." Curious, White Hawk hid and watched and waited. His patience was rewarded when he heard beautiful sounds coming from the sky and then watched as an object descended to earth. He described the object as a "basket" and reported that it was carrying a dozen "maidens."

And in 1663, a Jesuit priest in New France noted in his journal that he had seen "fiery serpents . . . flying through mid-air, borne on the wings of flame" which "seemed to issue from the Moon's bosom, with a noise like that of Cannon or Thunder." Then, as the priest watched, the mysterious object ascended until it disappeared from sight.

More than a century later, near Landing Lake, Manitoba, explorer David Thompson watched as "a meteor of globular form" descended from the sky, seeming to fly toward him and his men. At the last minute, the object changed course and crashed onto the ice of an adjacent frozen river, making a sound like a "mass of jelly." The craft smashed into "innumerable luminous pieces" after which it "instantly expired." The next morning, Thompson and his party investigated the crash site, but they found absolutely no indication that anything out of the ordinary had taken place there. It should be noted that David Thompson was known as an extremely careful note taker.

These historical reports seem to support the theory that UFOs have created crop circles when they land on Earth's fields. Despite this, most modern-day formations have been proven to be hoaxes, but can they all be written off as such? Perhaps only time will tell.

6

No Hex
Like an Old Hex

The Subway Mummy

Sadly, even back in 1975, seeing a badly dressed 15-year-old boy from an impoverished background in a Toronto subway station was a common enough sight to be barely worthy of comment. It's strange then that one such boy's presence in the St. George station of the university subway line created such a stir that year. The story was reported in newspapers across Canada, and readers responded to those articles with emotionally charged letters to editors. Of course, the fact that this lad, Nakht by name, lived and died more than 3,200 years ago no doubt explains the depth of curiosity.

Nakht's tomb was discovered in 1905, and his mummy was brought to Canada by Charles Currelly, the director of the then-fledgling Royal Ontario Museum (ROM). Right from the beginning, archaeologists and Egyptologists were intrigued by the contradiction between Nakht's humble position as a weaver and the trouble taken to preserve his body. Despite this point of interest, the mummy lay tucked away in a basement storage room at the museum for nearly 70 years. Then the remains were provided to an international team of medical specialists intent on examining the corpse in the hopes of gaining insight into ancient illnesses.

After the examination was completed, the mummy was to be moved from the ROM to the Museum for the History of Medicine in Toronto. Before that move was made, however, someone in authority apparently thought that the public should have the opportunity to see the unusual artifact. The deceased boy's remains were placed, Sleeping Beauty–like, in a glass case and positioned against a wall on the subway platform.

Unfortunately, a few subway passengers were frightened of the body's presence. Some remembered instances where disturbed bodies had carried hexes with them. The case most often cited was a reasonably recent one. Just 11 years before, Mohammed Ibrahim, the director of antiquities in Egypt, had fought hard to prevent a collection of Tutankhamun's relics from being shipped to Paris for an exhibition. After four months of arguing his case, Ibrahim finally agreed to have the antiquities sent to France.

He'd no sooner relented than his daughter was seriously

injured in a car accident. Badly shaken by the "coincidence," he informed Parisian officials that he'd changed his mind and would not be sending the articles for display. But the person he was speaking to would not accept this change in plans and insisted that Ibrahim keep his word. The Egyptian was so distressed about this turn of events that he left his office to take a walk and clear his mind. Seconds later, he was hit by a car and killed.

Torontonians who knew more about Egyptology pointed out that Mohammed Ibrahim was only the most recent victim of the curse of Tutankhamun; when the tomb was opened in 1922 there was a series of sudden and inexplicable deaths. A radiologist sent to investigate the tomb died en route to his assignment. A photographer associated with the investigation went blind and died shortly after. A scholar who'd been interested in the tomb investigation killed himself. Archaeologist Howard Carter's assistant, Richard Bethell, carried a vase from the tomb and shortly after died unexpectedly. The man who received that vase, Lord Westbury, killed himself soon after. The hearse carrying Westbury's body to the graveyard struck and killed an eight-year-old boy. How tragic that no one who saw that stolen vase hadn't heeded the words written on it: "Death shall come on swift wings to him that toucheth the tomb of Pharoah."

Lord Carnarvon, who had financed the expedition, was bitten on the neck by a mosquito, despite the fact that the area of the tomb was arid and thought to be mosquito-free.

By the following day, Carnarvon was critically ill, and he died 10 days later. By the oddest coincidence, all the lights in Cairo went out at the exact moment of his death and stayed out for five minutes. No one was ever able to explain that blackout.

Until 1925, Tutankhamun's corpse remained just as it had been found, wrapped in its original bandages, but when it was finally unwrapped, examiners found evidence that the pharaoh had also been bitten on the neck by a mosquito—in exactly the same place as Lord Carnarvon had been.

People who wanted Nakht's body removed from the subway were concerned about this apparently deadly history. They pointed out how foolish it was, under these circumstances, to place a mummy in an underground venue entirely dependent on electricity. They also found it curious that so much trouble had been taken to preserve a boy of such low social standing and worried that this seeming contradiction could be an indication that Nakht was, in some way, very special.

Edmund S. Meltzer, a scientist from the University of Toronto, reminded those concerned about a curse that many of the people involved with the 1922 Tutankhamun expedition had gone on to live long and fruitful lives. He also informed any frightened subway riders that stories about curses associated with the expedition only came to light after competing English newspapers discovered that the *London Times* had been granted exclusive rights to the story. Meltzer's more informed perspective assured most folks. It also illustrated that the possibility of a curse was, indirectly, a curse in itself.

Despite all the excitement caused by Nakht's presence in the Toronto subway station, there's no record of any calamities occurring during his stay. Nakht has remained on permanent display at Toronto's Academy of Medicine in their Museum for the History of Medicine ever since, without anything untoward occurring.

A Priest's Prophecy

Pity the innocent sailor serving aboard a cursed ship. Why, that curse could last for an entire voyage—or even longer. Could it last a lifetime? Or perhaps even beyond a person's natural life and into the eternity that is death? This seems to be the case in the following story.

In the fall of 1755, thousands of French settlers were expelled from Acadia. Most fled with only their lives. Others, however, had additional responsibilities. A man named LeBlanc, for instance, desperately wanted to save his daughter, Celeste, and the parish priest needed to save his church's valuable religious ornaments. Both men pleaded with the captain of *Tourmente*, a ship anchored in the Minas Basin, to sail their beloved treasures to safety in Quebec City.

The men's choice was not a wise one. *Tourmente*'s captain had a well-deserved reputation as a dishonest man. The eastbound voyage had barely begun when the captain seized the church's artifacts for himself and hurled the priest over-board, foolishly laughing at the religious man's final words, "Heaven will visit punishment upon all aboard the vessel for the sacrilege committed."

Seconds later, a single cloud appeared in the sky and a gale-force wind blew up. Above the ship, thunder boomed, lightning crackled, and yet the waters remained eerily calm. Still, the supernatural storm was too much for *Tourmente* and her crew. The once-proud ship was smashed to bits, and all aboard were killed.

Worse, their cursed fate didn't end there; for more than 200 years, people fishing off the coast of Nova Scotia have occasionally glimpsed a strange and frightening sight. Even on the calmest of nights, the image of an old-fashioned ship struggling against a torrential storm has been reported. The distressed vessel is encircled in an undulating blue glow that illuminates the figures of those who were aboard *Tourmente* on that fateful night. Her crew can be seen scurrying about the deck in obvious anxiety. And on the bow, away from the sailors, there is a lone figure: the spectre of a young woman wringing her hands and straining her eyes searching for some faint sign of safety.

The priest's hex must have been forever.

Family Ties

In 1664, Britain's King Charles II rewarded soldier William Craven by granting him the title 1st Earl of Craven. This distinction, the right to use the title "Earl," was to be passed down through generations of the Craven family, whose ancestral home was Morewood House in Hamstead Marshall, Berkshire. The 1st Earl of Craven died in 1697 at the age of 91, after having lived an active—some might say too active—life. William Craven apparently had an affair with one of his servants, Harriette Wilson. When he terminated this relationship, Harriette didn't slip away quietly into the night. She not only published all the lurid details of the affair in her memoirs but also hexed the earl's successors to suffer premature death.

The 2nd and 3rd earls died in their 50s. William George Robert Craven, the 4th earl, died at the age of 35 under questionable circumstances during a rowdy shipboard party. The 5th earl died at 35 of peritonitis, while the 6th earl succumbed to leukemia when he was 47. Thomas Craven, the 7th earl, suffered from depression and eventually took his own life at the age of 26.

At that point the family, understandably, sold Morewood House, but apparently that didn't lay the hex to rest because Dr. Robert Reid, the man who bought the property, killed himself shortly after taking residence. Worse, Simon Craven, the late Thomas Craven's younger brother, who had become the 8th earl, was killed at the age of 28. He was driving alone along a strip of road by the seaside near Eastbourne, Sussex, at 2:00 A.M. on August 30, 1990, when his car veered into a line of parked cars. No other details were released about the tragedy, but many presume that it was caused by the servant's hex.

Benjamin Robert Joseph Craven, born in 1989, is the 9th Earl of Craven. At this writing in 2010, he is 21 years of age and full of life. Despite the family's tragic history, they categorically deny the existence of Harriette Wilson's proclaimed curse.

Titanic Concerns

A longstanding legend holds that when RMS *Titanic* left Southampton, England, on April 10, 1912, it was carrying a cursed Egyptian mummy. According to this folklore, it was this curse that damned the enormous ship's maiden voyage. No one has ever been able to prove this, however, and by now the story is usually dismissed as no more than myth. What cannot be dismissed quite so easily, though, are the eerie similarities between the story of *Titanic* and a novel published 14 years before the historic tragedy.

Morgan Robertson, a moderately successful writer in the late 1800s, crafted a short novel entitled *Futility* that was based on a dreamlike vision he claimed came to him in a trance. The plot revolved around a ship named SS *Titan*, which set out from the United States bound for the United Kingdom. Robertson's fictional ship was the largest and most luxurious one ever built. It offered every possible advantage and safety measure to its 2,500 wealthy passengers. For that reason, it was considered unsinkable and

Did the *Titanic*'s tragic legacy actually begin before she sailed into infamy on April 10, 1912? This photograph shows the massive ship under construction in Belfast.

GEORGE GRANTHAM BAIN COLLECTION, LIBRARY OF CONGRESS 3A27541

therefore lacked an adequate number of lifeboats. During one night in April, when the ship was travelling faster than it should have been, the *Titan* struck an iceberg in the North Atlantic not far from Newfoundland. Nearly half the passengers drowned.

All these details are familiar because, in reality, the most famous, or infamous, shipwreck in the world is *Titanic*, the largest and most luxurious ship of its era. While travelling too fast, *Titanic* hit an iceberg near Newfoundland during the night of April 14, 1912. She was widely considered to be "nearly unsinkable," and partly for this reason, was inadequately equipped with lifeboats. As a result of that shortage, more than half her 2,223 passengers drowned.

Trance or no trance, how could Morgan Robertson have written a story that so closely paralleled that of the *Titanic* 14 years before the real ship's maiden voyage? Even the names of the ships are eerily similar. Could all variations of the name "Titanic" be hexed, or was Morgan Robertson's novella something of a literary hoax?

Consider this report from the *Prince Edward Island Patriot* on July 15, 1880, 18 years before Robertson's book was published and 32 years before the sailing and sinking of *Titanic*:

SUNK BY AN ICEBERG

STRANGE STORY OF THE LOSS OF A SHIP

AND THE COWARDLY ABANDONMENT OF

HER OWNER BY THIS CAPTAIN AND CREW

The Titania, sailing ship, Captain Lloyd, master, owned by John Rees, of Swansea, left St. John's for Miramachi [*sic*] in ballast on Tuesday morning last. Shortly before midnight, under cover of dense obscuring fog, the Titania struck with a terrific crash on a huge ice island and in a few hours sunk deep down in its wake. As soon as the vessel was known to be irretrievably wrecked Captain Lloyd ordered the [life] boats to be lowered away. The crew were all got safely out of the ship and all available provisions and stores secured to meet possible contingencies.

THE OWNER LEFT TO SINK

Mr. Rees, the owner, who was on board and had a considerable sum of money in his possession, got into the smaller boat, and placed, it is said, away aft in her this money and all his personal property that time availed him to save. Having forgotten something of importance he again boarded the sinking ship and, strangely enough, was deserted in his hour of peril by the crews of the two boats and left to sink with the sinking ship. The deep damnation of his taking off is to-day the subject of judicial investigation. No coherent story of the cowardly and highly criminal desertion of the owner of the Titania has been offered as yet by the captain or crew. The ship, after the collision, remained above water for nearly three hours. The sea was almost tranquil. A brisk breeze had but recently sprung up and the distance of the ship from the harbor of St. John was barely forty miles in a southeasterly direction.

THE CREW SAVED

Next morning at six o'clock, when about fifteen miles from the scene of disaster, the fishing schooner P.L. Whitton, returning from St. Johns' to the Grand Banks, fell in with two boats' crews, all well, took them on board and brought them safely to St. Johns' last night. No trace, however, of the money of the unfortunate Rees has been found.

UNSATISFACTORY EXPLANATIONS

When Captain Lloyd was interrogated as to the reason of his not waiting for or attempting to rescue Rees he replied that he was a very powerful man, and he feared to board the ship lest he should fling him overboard. No two individuals from the ill-fated Titania reproduce the same or even a consistent account of the unhappy occurrence. It is not surprising, therefore, that a dark cloud of suspicion has settled on the whole affair, and that a challenge not to be ignored has been addressed to the judicial authorities of Newfoundland to probe the matter to the bottom.

The parallels running through these three stories are chilling. We can never know for certain, but clearly Morgan Robertson's book could well have been based not on a vision that came to him while in a trance but instead on the 1880 sinking of *Titania*. By now it's impossible to know what factors were at work influencing the eerie coincidences, but hoax, hex or neither, it seems prudent not to book a cruise on any ship named in honour of the elder gods, the Titans! That good advice notwithstanding, sometimes what might seem like a hex is actually just a hoax, and this seems to be the case with an incident involving the tramp steamer *Titanian*.

At 11:00 P.M. on April 23, 1935, William C. Reeves was serving as a deckhand aboard *Titanian* as it approached Newfoundland. Perhaps young William was a lad of great imagination, or perhaps anyone would have noticed the coincidences of the time of year and the name and location of the vessel and been able to weave a pretty good tale around the situation. Perhaps truthfully or possibly just for dramatic flair, Reeves even added that he was reading

Morgan Robertson's novel *Futility* when a sixth sense apparently triggered a feeling of impending doom. Not wanting to alarm everyone unnecessarily, he remained quiet until he could resist the impulse no longer and cried out, "Stop the engines quickly! Iceberg ahead!" The men in the engine room lost no time responding to Reeves' shouts, and as the ship slowed they were shocked to see large chunks of ice floating dead ahead. When *Titanian* finally came to a complete stop, an enormous iceberg lay directly in its path.

Had William C. Reeves' intuition saved *Titanian* from falling victim to whatever hex had sunk *Titanic* and the fictional *Titan* in that very spot? No doubt that is exactly what Mr. Reeves wanted people to believe. Unfortunately, the truth of the matter is that *Titanian* was actually a good distance away from those fateful co-ordinates when it approached the icebergs, so this incident was simply a hoax—a sailor's attempt at revisionist history. Even so, the tale does provide further reason to stay off any ship with a name similar to *Titanic* in the North Atlantic near Newfoundland in April. After all, why tempt fate?

Triskaidekaphobia

Hexes have frequently been attached to numbers, but the number 13 is usually seen as the most unlucky. A man named W.E. Stephenson of Moose Jaw, Saskatchewan, had a dramatic encounter with that number on December 13, 1926, when he was defeated in his bid to serve another term as an alderman. His nomination had come on November 13 at a gathering of 13 politicians where Stephenson had been the 13th person to enter the room. There were 13 polling stations in the city and 13 candidates on the ballot. At the two polls located in the city hall where Stephenson was eager to work, he received a total of 13 votes. Citywide, W.E. Stephenson lost his bid for re-election by 13 votes.

Thirteen isn't the only number that can be problematic. The *Vancouver Sun* ran a thought-provoking article in its July 17, 1921, edition. An unnamed reporter described a strange situation involving a taxicab identified by the number 126. Although the cab was described as being "a splendid car" that had "always been driven by careful drivers," it had become known as "the car of fate"—and no wonder. It had been involved in eight "mishaps" over a period of only two years. It had "smashed headlong into the span on Cambie Street bridge," "killed a man in front of the John L. Sullivan Café," injured several people in an "accident on the Main Street hill" and most recently had, embarrassingly, crashed into the ditch near the Brighouse Racetrack while carrying a full complement of seven women passengers.

Of course, there have been other cars that seemed to have been hexed. The car that actor James Dean was driving when he died in a flaming crash was said to have been jinxed, and Stephen King's fictional car, Christine, was a pretty scary vehicle too. Thank goodness it was only a figment of that author's imagination—we hope.

7

Spooky Spots

Doomed

Even before European contact, the Cree and the Blackfoot were sworn enemies. Their history is rife with stories of battles between the two groups, and their relations were damaged even further when the Cree aligned themselves with the Mounties.

Shortly after North West Mounted Police inspector Cecil Denny was posted to Fort Walsh, in what is now Saskatchewan, he took some time off to explore his new surroundings. Denny was rafting along Battle Creek when a severe rainstorm hit. The sky went black, rain teemed down and vicious winds swirled around him. Soon thunder and lightning hit. The inspector realized that staying on the water would be life threatening. He made his way to shore and took shelter within a grove of trees.

When the intensity of the storm had abated somewhat, Denny began to walk a little farther from the creek. He hadn't gone very far before he heard voices and drums and chanting. The sounds had to mean that there was a group of Cree not too far away. He knew he could count on them for temporary shelter, food and warm, dry clothing.

Denny followed the sounds through the rain-soaked brush until he came to a clearing where a gathering of Cree families were happily going about their day, oblivious to the fierce storm that had driven him to shore. This struck the inspector as very odd, but stranger still, there was a very good reason why they were oblivious to the inclement weather: it was a beautiful summer's day where they were— warm and sunny—even though they were only a few metres away from where Denny stood, cold and soaking wet.

Badly confused by the idyllic scene being played out before him, Denny stood silently and watched until the intense rainstorm raging around him beat down even harder. He had to get into the proper shelter that the Cree tents would offer.

Denny darted toward the clearing. As he did, he was assaulted by a strange force of blue light that threw him to the ground. The next thing he knew, he was regaining consciousness; he must have been knocked out. He shook his head, clambered to his feet and rubbed his eyes. He was staring at the clearing, but now there was no sign of the encampment that he was sure he'd seen just moments before. He was stranded—by weather and time and space, it seemed. He headed back to Fort Walsh on foot and arrived hours later, cold, hungry and tired but grateful to be safe at last.

The next morning when he told his colleagues about his experience, no one believed him. Despite that, Denny knew that he wouldn't be able to put his mind at rest until he examined the anomalous area again, and so, using the excuse that he needed to retrieve the supplies he'd left behind, Denny made his way back to the clearing.

He found that the storm had done considerable damage, but there was absolutely no sign that there'd been a recent encampment there. More confused than ever, Denny began to probe more carefully. This time his hunt was rewarded. He found proof that the area had been inhabited at one time—a very long time ago.

It wasn't until he related his story to a Native guide that Denny was finally able to at least begin to understand his experience during the storm. It seemed that many years before, a party of Blackfoot had sneaked up on a Cree camp and killed every man, woman and child. Legend has it that the slaughter had left the area hexed, and that when the atmosphere is charged with electricity, as it was during that severe thunderstorm, the victims' images reappear.

Inspector Denny recorded this information in great

detail, but unfortunately didn't leave us with his reaction to his experience in that hexed clearing.

Truth Be Told

In 1985, a small, Toronto-based publisher, Hounslow Press, released a book called *Ghost Stories of Canada*, written by Val Clery. It was a short book—little more than 100 pages long—but it contained 11 chilling, well-told tales set in various Canadian locations. The writing style was lively, as if the author had first-hand knowledge of each supernatural tale. Some of Clery's finest writing, however, went into the concluding paragraph of the book's cryptically worded introduction.

> But are these stories true? In the shadowy half-world shared by imagination and memory, by fear and longing and doubt, where stories are exchanged by whispered word of mouth, there is no truth. Nothing is certain, nothing can be proved, nothing is real—these are ghost stories.

Those evocatively worded phrases were no doubt designed to perplex—and perplex they did. Were these stories merely figments of Clery's imagination, or were they, as the tone of the book implied, chronicles that he had collected over the years? Neither librarians nor booksellers knew. Where should the book be shelved? With fiction or non-fiction? Who knew? And after a while, who cared? The book was easy, entertaining reading, but one tale,

"The Slaughter," was especially intriguing. Clery relates the saga as if he and his former colleague, Andy Mckee, were standing together on the banks of Saskatchewan's Souris River, not far from the Canada-US border.

The land had been granted to Andy's grandfather in appreciation of his dedication to quelling the Metis uprising in the 1880s. Fighting the Catholic Metis apparently came easily to Mckee, who was a devoted Orangeman, an Irish Protestant immigrant.

The homestead wasn't much of a prize, however. The only fertile portion was "bottomland," a gully near the river, where to Mckee's dismay, he found a family of Metis squatters. Mckee handled the situation in a very permanent way before moving his wife and baby son to the property. A few weeks later, his wife died. The child, Andy Mckee's father, was raised on the land and, like his father before him, married, had a son and lost his wife at a young age.

This meant that three generations of Mckee men lived on a piece of property that would barely produce a crop. It was a confined and bleak childhood for young Andy, made even more restricted by the fact that his grandfather wouldn't allow anyone to set foot on the land near the river.

By the time Andy was in his teens, drought and the Depression had devastated the Canadian prairies. By then, his grandfather was an unstable old man, and his father was an unemployed miner. Andy's world was small and ugly. One hot August afternoon, he escaped that harsh reality the only way he could—by disobeying his grandfather's order to stay away from the fertile soil of the bottomland.

The moment he stepped into the gully, Andy knew he'd made a mistake. Everything about the place felt evil. Shivers so strong they were nearly convulsions wracked his body, while his shirt was soaked with sweat from the unrelenting sun. A malevolent force encompassed him. Finally, he managed to struggle to the relative safety of his grandfather's old house.

That night, Andy tossed and turned with terrifying dreams about the evil that had engulfed him. The next morning he found his grandfather dead at the kitchen table. Now there was just Andy and his father. Worse, winter was closing in, and if they couldn't find coal they'd freeze to death. The elder Mckee told his son that the coal seams along the riverbank were their only hope. Andy begged his father to think of another solution. He confessed that he'd disobeyed and trespassed onto the bottomland and that the very air at that place was hexed. He didn't think it was a coincidence that the old man had died that night.

Andy's father didn't listen, nor did he come back from his search for coal. Andy found his body on the bottomland. He tried to bury the corpse, but the evil oozing from the hexed land was too strong. Suddenly he realized how his grandfather had dealt with the Metis squatters who had been camping near the river on his homestead those many years before: he had shot and killed the entire family.

Terrified by the obvious power of the curse, Andy turned and ran. He made it to Estevan on foot and stayed there until he'd saved enough from odd jobs to take the train to Toronto. He hadn't been back to the hexed property where he was raised until that afternoon when, as a middle-aged man, he stood on the homestead with author Val Clery.

Now that is one dramatic tale: land hexed so badly by both bad blood and cold blood that its legacy killed two men and drove a third as far away as he could go. But is there really a cursed piece of land near the Saskatchewan–North Dakota border? Although *Ghost Stories of Canada* is often mistaken for similarly titled, non-fiction books, there is every indication that the hex was a hoax and that Clery's stories are works of fiction.

Hell Fire Cat

A visit to Dublin, Ireland, wouldn't be complete without a hike up Montpelier Hill. The view of the city from the hill is absolutely breathtaking, perhaps only surpassed by the crumbling ruins of Montpelier House, which stand at the summit.

The Right Honourable William Connolly, who built the place in 1725, must have felt very lucky when he found this site. The view was spectacular, and there were even potential construction materials—a standing stone and boulders from a prehistoric burial cairn. He set to work breaking up and incorporating the chunks of stone into his new structure.

Unfortunately, Connolly either didn't know or didn't care that those boulders had been placed there very carefully and purposefully. The spot had long been an ancient pagan site of worship, perhaps similar in purpose to Stonehenge. Connolly had not only desecrated a sacred area but had even incorporated the large rocks into his building.

Dubliners watched in horror as the work on Montpelier House progressed. They had always shown deference for the ancient site and given it a wide berth. They were sure that nothing good could come from Connolly's disrespectful project, and apparently their misgivings were warranted, for no sooner had the home been finished than a storm blew the roof off. Nearby residents were sure it was an act of vengeance by the original and long-dead builders. Rumours immediately began to circulate that the place was cursed.

Connolly, however, was undeterred. He re-engineered and rebuilt the roof so that this time it was, according to the 1912 publication *Neighbourhoods of Dublin*, "of impregnable strength." The new roof might have been sturdy but the locals weren't appeased. They feared that nothing could change the fact that the building stood on ground that their ancestors had considered hallowed.

If Montpelier House wasn't already seriously tainted by that time, it was certainly well on its way. Then, in 1735, Richard Parsons, the 1st Earl of Rosse, took possession of the place. Parsons was a proud member of the infamous Hell Fire Club—a group of men who spent their leisure time mocking the Roman Catholic Church. Their rituals included black magic that often involved both the sacrifice and the worship of black cats.

The Hell Fire Club's bizarre services continued until 1740, when the building was abandoned. It has never been occupied since. Today, Montpelier House is owned by the Irish government and is open to the public; however, most visitors are tourists, since those who know the eerie ruin's history also know that it is haunted by that most recognized symbol of a hex: the spectre of an enormous black cat.

Talbot's Toll

It goes without saying that the purpose of a lighthouse is to prevent accidents and deaths. How ironic then that the first lighthouse built on the Canadian side of Lake Superior was implicated in the deaths of its first three keepers.

Construction of the white tower on Talbot Island, near Superior's north shore and west of Marathon, Ontario, began in the summer of 1867. Installed in the tower was a fixed-beam light, much simpler to build than a rotating beacon, and the project went along as smoothly as expected. There were absolutely no hints of the tragedies that were to come.

There was no shipping during Lake Superior's icy winters, which meant that the lighthouse would only have to be maintained for three seasons. For this reason, come November of that first year, the lighthouse keeper, a man named Perry, boarded his small, open boat and headed for shore. He didn't make it—at least not alive. His body was found the following spring, washed up on the shore near Nipigon. Authorities presumed that the poor man had frozen to death trying to make it to safety.

A few weeks later, a man named Thomas Lamphier moved to the tiny island and brought his wife with him for both help and companionship. Lamphier was an experienced seaman, and his wife was familiar with the area, so the two seemed to be ideally suited to the job.

The Lamphiers had heard about their predecessor's fate and therefore intended to live on the lonely island all year round. They did so until Thomas took ill. They were completely isolated from medical assistance, and within a few weeks Thomas died. His wife was devastated by the loss of her husband and also by the overwhelming challenge of surviving by herself.

No help arrived until spring, and when it did, those who found her were shocked at Mrs. Lamphier's state. She had become an old woman in just a matter of months. The rescuers pulled Thomas' remains from the cavern where his wife had put him, as she was unable to bury him on the rocky island and had feared that wildlife would be attracted to the decaying body. Then they ferried the widow away from the desolate rock that had held her captive for so many months.

Once news of the Lamphiers' fate became known among those in the nautical community, there were whispers that the island was jinxed. Some referred to the light as "the lighthouse of doom." Despite this, by the spring of 1872, the government was able to find a replacement keeper, Andrew Hynes.

Like Perry five years before, Hynes closed up the lighthouse in November and set out for shore in an open boat. For eight tortuous days, Hynes fought storms and freezing cold. Miraculously, he made it to shore, but by the time he did he was barely alive. Hynes never recovered from the horrendous trip and died a short time later.

After that, no one would take a posting at the Talbot Island lighthouse, and it was abandoned. The building has long since succumbed to the ravages of Lake Superior, but the island's reputation as a cursed outcropping of land has never been forgotten.

The Hexed Ruin

There's something inherently creepy about a deserted, derelict building—so much so that exploring such an abandoned house can become an important rite of passage for neighbourhood children. It's reasonable to assume that youngsters living near Montreal's Mount Royal must have had hours of spine-tingling excitement sneaking about in the dilapidated McTavish mansion. Spookier still, the house was never completely finished and so had never been lived in.

The enormous structure has been gone since 1839, so it's understandable that some details of its history have become lost or confused, and the accuracy of those that remain are probably questionable at best. Even so, this is a classic tale of a hexed property. We just can't know for certain which of the nightmarish stories were caused by McTavish's spirit and which were invented by generations of people after him—all with very vivid imaginations.

In 1763, at the age of 13, Simon McTavish left his home in Scotland for the excitement of the New World. He was an intelligent and industrious fur trader and soon became the wealthiest person in the city of Montreal. Not surprisingly, he wanted to build a family home that reflected that status. This was an ambitious, expensive and time-consuming undertaking. Sadly, he never saw his dream completed. He died of pneumonia in 1804. Rumours of his restless spirit roaming Mount Royal began immediately.

In 1892, an unnamed writer described a macabre event that he or she maintained had happened in the McTavish mansion and that supposedly led to the man's death. What the story lacks in accuracy it certainly makes up for in its colourful presentation.

According to this tale, one night Simon McTavish experienced a sudden strong urge to visit his property. At the time, his wife and four children were away in Scotland. Workers had the house completely framed in by that time, and it's said that when he looked up to inspect the roof, he was horrified to see the image of his beloved wife hanging from a beam. Another author, Edgar Andrew Collard, maintains that the dreadful vision was so real and terrifying to McTavish that he ordered all work on the house to stop until the next mail ship arrived from the British Isles. When it did, the man's worst fears were confirmed. A letter informed him that at exactly the moment he'd seen the awful mirage, his wife had, in fact, hanged herself. The devastated man also hanged himself or died soon after of a broken heart.

While this is an undeniably spooky and highly romantic tale—that's absolutely all it is. McTavish died of pneumonia, and his wife outlived him. Yet somehow the legend persisted and was included in a book published 150 years later.

According to another legend, the slope of Mount Royal is hexed by Simon McTavish's restless spirit. At first glance, this story seems completely preposterous, but with sufficient digging, the origins of the tale become clear. Collard writes that in the 1820s, people claimed to have seen the ghost of Simon McTavish sliding down the side of Mount Royal. Depending on who was telling the tale, he was using either his coffin or the lid of his coffin as a toboggan! Given that there's no record of this man indulging in such lighthearted activities, the scenario's more than a bit perplexing—until you learn that students at McGill Medical School, located down the hill from the Mount Royal Cemetery, had to obtain cadavers illegally. It's not much of a stretch to imagine someone associated with the medical faculty robbing graves and then transporting the ill-gotten corpses down the mountain on some sort of a sled. A few folks went so far as to say that it was the grave robbers themselves who started circulating that particular story.

The reality surrounding the final demise of both McTavish's property and his family is considerably more tragic than this whimsical tale. One of McTavish's children died at age 25, two others at 21, and his daughter Ann died while still in her teens. It was commonly said that the mansion must have been cursed right from the beginning, and if that was so, the hex continued right to the very end of the huge home's existence. In 1839, while the crumbling mansion was being demolished, a worker fell three storeys to his death.

Edgar Andrew Collard completed his description of the events in these words: "Those who had always believed that a sinister spirit hovered over the mansion must have thought this last tragedy a fitting end to its story."

A Reverse Hex?

While conducting interviews for her books in the *Ghost Stories of Saskatchewan* series, author Jo-Anne Christensen came across a cemetery where one particular grave enjoyed a kind of reverse hex. Christensen describes the graveyard as being in a small town in southern Saskatchewan and the marker for this grave as "nondescript."

One of the cemetery caretaker's responsibilities was to clear away bouquets left by friends and relatives once the flowers were wilted and past their prime. A particular grave required considerably less attention than others. Day after day, the caretaker would go back and check the flowers left beside that tombstone, but they were always as fresh and pretty as they were the day before. This strange situation began to worry the man. He explained, "I was cutting a bit of a wide berth around the grave, because I just didn't know what to make of it."

Finally, the man had the good fortune to run into one of the cemetery's previous employees, who told him, "That's just the way it is on that grave. When she gets flowers, don't even bother checking them for a month or two. They just stay fresh."

Christensen goes on to explain that in the three years the caretaker worked in that cemetery, "he found the strange phenomenon to be absolutely consistent, and never discovered a logical explanation."

Is there such a thing as the opposite of a hex? Perhaps we know such a phenomenon as a blessing.

CHAPTER

8

Sports and Entertainment Hexes

Hockey Hexes

In 1940, after beating the Toronto Maple Leafs in a six-game final series, the New York Rangers jubilantly hoisted the Stanley Cup at Madison Square Garden. After the on-ice celebrations were through, the team retired to their dressing room. Rangers' president John Kilpatrick was over the moon with the excitement of the win, especially because the organization had just paid off the mortgage on their home rink. He decided to initiate the ultimate mortgage-burning party by placing the paid-in-full documents in the bowl of the Stanley Cup and setting the papers on fire.

At the time, there were those who were uncomfortable with the ritual burning ceremony, feeling that Kilpatrick had desecrated hockey's Holy Grail. They worried that the president's actions might have been disrespectful to the heritage of the Stanley Cup and that he might have unwittingly put the team's future successes in jeopardy. Others thought that such superstitions were utter silliness—and that latter group might have been correct, except that the New York Rangers didn't win the Stanley Cup again for more than 50 years.

By play-off time in 1994, it looked as though the curse's grasp might have weakened, for the team had systematically eliminated their crosstown rivals, the Islanders, before also beating the Washington Capitals. It wasn't until the Rangers faced the New Jersey Devils that the team faltered. Was the association between the apparent curse and a team named the "Devils" a coincidence or an extension of the hex? People wondered. Even the press was asked if the Rangers would ever be free of the fallout from John Kilpatrick's unintentionally foolhardy act so many decades before.

In the end, it took a Canadian hockey player, former Edmonton Oiler Mark Messier, to defeat the Devils by scoring a hat trick in the seventh game of the semi-final series. Finally the Rangers would advance to play for all the marbles. Better still, their opponents were the Vancouver Canucks, a team that hadn't had a stellar year. Despite their regular-season record, the Canucks gave the Rangers a serious run for their money in the first game and ended up beating the New York team in overtime.

The Rangers, led by "the Moose," Mark Messier, rallied though and won the next three games. This meant they could win the Stanley Cup on home ice in game five. But they didn't. Vancouver won the fifth game and the sixth as well. It looked as though the hex was holding.

Game seven was back in Madison Square Garden, where the hex had begun 54 years before. Both teams played well, and with just seconds to go in regular time, the Rangers were up 3 to 2. A Canuck player fired a deadly shot at the net, but the puck hit the goalpost and bounced clear. When the final buzzer sounded, the New York Rangers had won the Stanley Cup. The curse had finally been lifted.

Six players on the victorious New York Rangers team were former Edmonton Oilers, and a total of 13 players on the roster were Canadians. The number 13 is usually considered to be bad luck, but it this case it proved to be just what was needed to finally nix the hex.

One hockey hex that hasn't been nixed dates back to the 1992 Stanley Cup playoffs. The Montreal Canadiens were down one goal to the Los Angeles Kings. In the dying minutes of the second game, perhaps thinking that he had nothing to lose, Montreal coach Jacques Demers protested that the Kings' Marty McSorley was playing with an illegal stick. Demers demanded that the blade be measured. The measurement proved that the coach had been around hockey long enough to correctly spot illegal equipment, and McSorley was given a two-minute penalty.

The veteran coach's strategy paid off. The Canadiens' Eric Desjardins scored to tie the game and force overtime. Desjardins was the only advantage the Montreal team needed. He also scored in overtime, clinched the game and then went on to help the Canadiens win the Stanley Cup. It seemed that the tide had turned the moment Coach Demers challenged McSorley's exaggeratedly curved stick—for that season anyway.

The years that followed, however, were not kind to Canada's teams in the NHL. At this writing, no Canadian team has won the Stanley Cup since. In 1994, the New York Rangers defeated the Vancouver Canucks. In 2004, the Tampa Bay Lightning beat the Calgary Flames. In 2006, it was the Carolina Hurricanes over the Edmonton Oilers. In 2007, the Anaheim Ducks ruined the Ottawa Senators' chance to hoist the coveted cup, and in 2010, the two Canadian teams in the conference semifinals, the Canucks and the Canadiens, were eliminated before the finals.

Did Demers' challenge jinx the Canadian teams? If so, then the Quebec Nordiques managed to find a way around the hex when they were moved to Denver and became the Colorado Avalanche. They won the Stanley Cup in 1996 and 2001.

Curling's Curse

American curler Bob LaBonte has something few other people have—or would want to have: he has a curse named after him. The story of this curse begins back in 1972, when the Air Canada Silver Broom Championship was held in Garmisch-Partenkirchen, Germany. It had been an exciting few days of curling. Canada was undefeated. The stakes and the tension were high for this final game against the United States. It was winner-take-all, and Canada trailed slightly.

Still, Canada's skip, Orest Meleschuk, was hopeful. He was confident in his team's ability, and most important, he had the hammer, or last rock. The two points he needed were within his grasp. It was going to be a tricky shot, but he'd made those before. The Americans had the rock closest to the centre button, but if Meleschuk could knock it out without overshooting his own, he would tie the game and then could go on to win with the hammer.

He made the hit, but from where he stood he couldn't be sure which team's rock lay closest to the button. American skip Bob LaBonte was in a better position to judge, and he was sure that his team had won. He jumped up in celebration. As he landed, though, the unthinkable happened: Bob LaBonte slipped and kicked the Canadian rock closer to the button. Canada was awarded two points. Then, adding insult to injury, the Canadians scored another point with the hammer.

An American journalist retrospectively referred to the incident and its fallout as a hex, thus creating the term "LaBonte Curse," because a team from North Dakota didn't make it to the world championships of curling again until 1997. Interestingly though, the LaBonte Curse also worked *against* Canada. No Canadian men's curling team won a world championship again until 1980.

Despite the costly gaffe, Bob LaBonte was the embodiment of the graceful loser, as he willingly and frequently shared anecdotes of the incident, clearly making himself, literally, the fall guy.

Pitching a Lot of Good

In 2004, a security guard with the Toronto Blue Jays Major League Baseball team told pitcher Miguel Batista that Toronto's award-winning ballpark, then called the SkyDome (now the Rogers Centre), had been built on the site of an ancient Native burial ground. Unfortunately, that security guard's name has been lost through the passage of years, but Batista's reaction to the man's disclosure remains.

No amount of research has ever turned up any written record verifying the guard's story, but the enormous lake-front property has been prime real estate since the last glacial retreat. Whether the story was true or merely an urban legend didn't matter to Batista. He was a spiritual man and was not in the least afraid that the legend meant the area was hexed. He was simply intrigued, because the day before he'd had what he referred to as a "freaky" experience.

It seems that in addition to being a professional athlete, Miguel Batista is also an accomplished musician. On that particular day in 2004, while the opposing team took the field for batting practice, the Jays' pitcher was playing his flute. Suddenly the instrument was knocked from his hands by an apparently invisible force. The pitcher took it as a sign from those who'd inhabited the area thousands of years before, and perhaps as a pre-emptive strike against the possibility of a hex, the pitcher-cum-flautist renewed his efforts as a benevolent citizen of the world and has become well known for his generosity and spirituality.

Hollywood Hex

When is a hex not a hex? Well, perhaps when spurious bits of information—mere coincidences really—are stitched together in such a way as to spin the facts. The much-talked about "Oscar hex" is a prime example. It's said that the winner of the best actress Academy Award will soon find her marriage or personal relationship in serious jeopardy.

Much attention was paid to this "hex" when Sandra Bullock won the award for her 2009 role as Leigh Anne Tuohy in *The Blind Side*. Almost immediately after the Academy Awards ceremony in March 2010, rumours began to surface that Bullock's husband, Jesse James, had been seeing several other women.

Was the so-called Oscar hex to blame? If so, does this mean that the best actress winner is then really the loser? Given that Hollywood marriages have never been known for their stability, surely the blame could lie with coincidental timing. A check back through the history of the Academy Awards might help clarify the situation.

Mary Pickford and Douglas Fairbanks were known as Hollywood's golden couple until Mary won the 1929 Oscar for best actress. Soon after this, their marriage disintegrated, causing heartbreak that neither Doug nor Mary ever fully recovered from. LIBRARY OF CONGRESS 30610

At the second Academy Awards ceremony, Mary Pickford, a Canadian, won the Academy Award for best actress of 1929 for her role in *Coquette*. She and Douglas Fairbanks had long been known as Hollywood's "golden couple," but shortly after Pickford's win, Fairbanks left her to marry his lover, Lady Sylvia Ashley. Pickford eventually remarried as well, but it's been widely reported that both she and Fairbanks regretted their separation for the rest of their lives. Was this the beginning of the Oscar hex?

The following year another Canadian, Norma Shearer, won for her role in *The Divorcee*. Oddly, despite the precedent set the previous year and the provocative title of the film, Shearer's marriage to Irving Thalberg remained solid until his untimely death at the age of 37. Shearer eventually married Martin Arrouge, but clearly she loved Thalberg to her dying day, as she was reported to have mistakenly called her new husband "Irving" on several occasions.

The following year, yet another Canadian was awarded the coveted best actress Oscar, but Marie Dressler, who won for her performance in *Min and Bill*, was unaffected. Helen Hayes also escaped the apparent hex after winning the award for *The Sin of Madelon Claudet* (1932).

Katharine Hepburn won the 1933 Oscar for *Morning Glory*, the first of her three Academy Awards. The following year she divorced Ludlow Ogden Smith, but it is well known that for nearly three decades her true love was Spencer Tracy.

Claudette Colbert and her husband, Norman Foster,

divorced the year after her 1934 win for *It Happened One Night*. It took Bette Davis' marriage a little longer to dissolve. She was awarded the 1935 Oscar for *Dangerous* and won again for the 1938 film *Jezebel*. She and Harmon Nelson divorced that year. French actress Luise Rainer was the first actress to win two years in a row, for *The Great Ziegfeld* (1936) and *The Good Earth* (1937), but her success might have destroyed her marriage to Clifford Odets in 1940.

Vivien Leigh's remarkable portrayal of Scarlett O'Hara in *Gone with the Wind* clinched the Academy's top honours for 1939. That year, she and Herbert Leigh Holman divorced, and Vivien immediately married Laurence Olivier. That marriage held through her award-winning role in *A Streetcar Named Desire*.

Ginger Rogers showed that she could act as well as dance and won the 1940 Oscar for *Kitty Foyle*. The next year, she and Lew Ayres were divorced. Joan Fontaine won for the 1941 Alfred Hitchcock film *Suspicion*; her marriage to Brian Aherne lasted until 1945. In 1942, Greer Garson played the title role in *Mrs. Miniver* and was divorced in 1947.

Jennifer Jones won the 1943 award for *The Song of Bernadette*. She and Robert Walker divorced in 1945, but the marriage failure likely had more to do with Jones' affair with David O. Selznick than her Oscar win. Joan Crawford's marriage to Phillip Terry ended a few months after she accepted the 1945 statuette for *Mildred Pierce*, and Jane Wyman's performance in *Johnny Belinda* earned her the 1948 Oscar and a divorce from future US president Ronald Reagan.

Olivia de Havilland's marriage survived her first Oscar win for *To Each His Own* (1946) but succumbed after she won again for the 1949 film *The Heiress*. Interestingly, Ingrid Bergman followed the same pattern with her wins for *Gaslight* (1944) and *Anastasia* (1956).

Elizabeth Taylor's marital history skews any attempt at statistical investigation and really puts her in a class by herself. She first won the best actress award in 1960 for *BUtterfield 8* and was divorced from Eddie Fisher in 1964. She won again in 1966, this time co-starring with her husband Richard Burton in *Who's Afraid of Virginia Woolf?* That marriage—her first to Burton—escaped the hex.

Julie Andrews' role in *Mary Poppins* earned her top honours for 1964. By 1967, she was no longer married to Tony Walton. Maggie Smith's marriage nearly made it to the five-years-after mark, but not quite. She won the 1969 Oscar for *The Prime of Miss Jean Brodie*, and her marriage to Robert Stephens ended in 1974. Jane Fonda and her husband Roger Vadim also divorced in 1974. She had won her first Academy Award for the 1971 film *Klute*. Fonda's second win, for *Coming Home* (1978), wasn't as destructive to her marital bliss with Tom Hayden, with whom she remained until 1990.

If a person wanted to accept the Oscar-hex theory, then Liza Minelli's 1972 win for *Cabaret* destroyed her marriage, as did Faye Dunaway's 1976 award for *Network* and Geraldine Page's win for the 1985 film *The Trip to Bountiful*. Marlee Matlin's marriage to William Hurt only lasted a year after she won an Oscar for her 1986 role in *Children of a Lesser God*.

Emma Thompson's marriage to Kenneth Branagh ended in 1995, only three years after she'd won for her portrayal of Margaret Schlegel in *Howards End*. Interestingly, Hilary Swank's marriage to Chad Lowe survived her 1999 win for *Boys Don't Cry*, even though she famously forgot to thank him in her acceptance speech. In 2004, when she won a second time, this time for *Million Dollar Baby*, Swank remembered to publicly acknowledge Lowe, but the bad luck hit anyway. Two years later, she and Lowe had gone their separate ways.

Halle Berry's marriage to Eric Benet ended in 2005. She'd won the 2001 best actress Oscar for *Monster's Ball*. Reese Witherspoon won the 2005 award for *Walk the Line*. Less than 24 months later, she was no longer married to Ryan Phillippe.

The missing years in this compilation are ones in which the woman who won the Academy Award for best actress didn't suffer a marriage breakup—at least not for the next five years. Using that criterion, 24 out of the 80 winners' relationships fell victim to the "hex." That ratio works out neatly to 30 per cent, so—you be the judge—is it the lifestyle of the rich and famous that's to blame for the marital instability or is the Oscar hex real?

Bibliography

Aykroyd, Peter H., with Angela Narth. *A History of Ghosts: The True Story of Seances, Mediums, Ghosts and Ghostbusters.* New York: Rodale Inc., 2009.

Bemister, Margaret. *Thirty Indian Legends.* Toronto: The Macmillan Company of Canada, 1912.

Billinghurst, Jane. *Grey Owl: The Many Faces of Archie Belaney.* Toronto: Greystone Books, 1999.

Boulton, Marsha. *The Just a Minute Omnibus: Glimpses of our Great Canadian Heritage.* Toronto: McArthur and Company, 2009.

Bradley, Mickey, and Dan Gordon. *Haunted Baseball: Ghosts, Curses, Legends and Eerie Events.* Guilford, CT: The Lyons Press, 2007.

Calgary Herald. December 31, 1935; October 25, 1956; November 8, 1956.

Christensen, Jo-Anne. *Ghost Stories of Saskatchewan 3.* Toronto: Dundurn Press, 2009.

———. *More Ghost Stories of Saskatchewan.* Edmonton: Lone Pine Publishing, 2000.

Clery, Val. *Ghost Stories of Canada.* Toronto: Hounslow Press, 1985.

Collard, Edgar Andrew. *Montreal Yesterdays.* Toronto: Longmans Canada, 1963.

———. *100 More Tales from All Our Yesterdays.* Montreal: The Gazette, 1990.

Crichton, Robert. *The Great Impostor.* New York: Random House, 1959.

Danielson, Vivian, and James White. *Bre-X: Gold Today, Gone Tomorrow.* Toronto: The Northern Miner, 1998.

Edwards, G.R. *Winnipeg Free Press,* September 28, 1963.

Fanthorpe, Lionel and Patricia. *Mysteries and Secrets of Time.* Toronto: Dundurn, 2007.

Halifax Herald. November 26, 1934.

Hennacy Powell, Diane. *The ESP Enigma: The Scientific Case for Psychic Phenomena.* New York: Walker and Company, 2009.

Hutchinson, Brian. *Fools' Gold: The Making of a Global Market Fraud.* Toronto: Alfred A. Knopf Canada, 1998.

Innes, Brian. *Fakes and Forgeries: The True Crime Stories of History's Greatest Deceptions.* London: Reader's Digest, 2005.

James, Rick. *The Ghost Ships of Royston.* Vancouver: Underwater Archaeological Society of British Columbia, 2004.

Jones, Richard. *Haunted Houses of Britain and Ireland.* London: New Holland Publishers, 2005.

Katsoulis, Melissa. *Literary Hoaxes: An Eye-Opening History of Famous Frauds.* New York: Sky Horse Publishing, 2009.

Ogden, Tom. *The Complete Idiot's Guide to Ghosts & Hauntings.* 2nd ed. New York: Penguin Group, 2004.

Poltergeists and the Paranormal. Leicestershire, England: Bookmart Ltd., 1993.

Prince Edward Island Patriot. July 15, 1880.

Reader's Digest. *How Did It Really Happen?* Montreal: Reader's Digest, 2000.

Roberts, David. *Great Exploration Hoaxes.* San Francisco: Sierra Club, 1982.

Smith, Donald B. *From the Land of Shadows: The Making of Grey Owl.* Saskatoon: Western Producer Prairie Books, 1990.

Bibliography

Stonehouse, Frederick. *Haunted Lakes II: More Great Lakes Ghost Stories*. Duluth: Lake Superior Port Cities Inc., 2000.

Telfer, Geordie. *Real Canadian Pirates: Buccaneers & Rogues of the North*. Edmonton: Folklore Publishing, 2007.

Vancouver Sun Weekend Magazine. October 22, 1955.

Walsh, Darryll. *Ghost Waters: Canada's Haunted Seas and Shores*. East Lawrencetown, NS: Pottersfield Press, 2002.

Wells, Jennifer. *Fever: The Dark Mystery of the Bre-X Gold Rush*. Toronto: Viking, 1998.

Wikipedia. "Bre-X;" "Ferdinand Waldo Demara."

Yes Magazine. *Hoaxed! Fakes and Mistakes in the World of Science*. Toronto: Kids Can Press, 2009.

Index

Index

Acknowledgements

Many thanks to those who supported this project: Rodger Touchie, Vivian Sinclair, Susan Adamson, Liesbeth Leatherbarrow, John Walls and everyone connected with the Amazing Stories series. My warmest thanks to the Amazing Stories series editor, Lesley Reynolds. Working with you has been a privilege.

Thanks also to W. Ritchie Benedict, researcher extraordinaire. Your diligence, especially under such difficult circumstances, was so appreciated. As always, thanks to my family. Without their love and support, my career would have been both impossible and pointless. Special thanks to my husband, Bob, for his hours of diligent proofreading.

photo by Robert Smith

About the Author

Barbara Smith is the bestselling author of *The Mad Trapper: Unearthing a Mystery*, the *Ghost Stories of Alberta* series, *Canadian Ghost Stories* and 20 other books, all sharing the theme of social history. She lives on Vancouver Island.